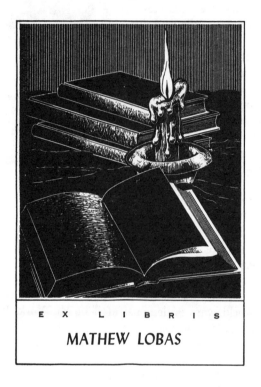

EX LIBRIS

*MATHEW LOBAS*

# FOREWORD

For years we fundamentalists have challenged our young people to pattern their life after a "real man". In Tom Skeyhill's book "Sergeant York", you find, near perfect form that real man we've been describing. We're impressed with his great shooting ability and courage in battle, but the character that was instilled in him by his mother and father was the real agent that led to his abilities in the field. This man was fashioned first in the home. That's where real men come from. Alvin York feared no man because he feared God. In Sergeant York is found the real American man in the truest sense. He embodies all we stand for. The integrity, hard work, nobility and manliness that shaped this nation and helped us win two world wars is demonstrated in Mr. York. When thinking of this leader of men, I think of David's words to Solomon, "Be strong therefore, and shew thyself a man." Every father should encourage his son to read this book. Would to God we had men like Alvin York today! I will read this book again.

Evangelist Tim Lee
Garland, TX

# SERGEANT YORK
## LAST OF THE LONG HUNTERS

# 13 Resolutions to Live By

*Age-old wisdom for a brand-new year.*

*by Jonathan Edwards*

*Being* sensible that I am unable to do anything without God's help, I do humbly entreat Him, by His grace, to enable me to keep these Resolutions, so far as they are agreeable to His will, for Christ's sake.

[I will] remember to read over these Resolutions once a week.

✠ Resolved, That I will do whatsoever I think to be most to the glory of God, and my own good, profit, and pleasure, in the whole of my duration; without any consideration of the time, whether now, or never so many myriads of ages hence. Resolved, to do whatever I think to be my duty, and most for the good and advantage of mankind in general.

✠ Resolved, Never to lose one moment of time, but to improve it in the most profitable way I possibly can.

✠ Resolved, to live with all my might, while I do live.

✠ Resolved, Never to do anything, which I would be afraid to do if it were the last hour of my life.

✠ Resolved, Never to do anything out of revenge.

✠ Resolved, Never to speak evil of any one, so that it shall tend to his dishonour, more or less, upon no account except for some real good.

✠ Resolved, To study the Scriptures so steadily, constantly, and frequently, as that I may find, and plainly perceive, myself to grow in the knowledge of the same.

✠ Resolved, Never to count that a prayer, nor to let that pass as a prayer, nor that as a petition of prayer, which is so made, that I cannot hope that God will answer it; nor that as a confession which I cannot hope God will accept.

✠ Resolved, to ask myself, at the end of every day, week, month and year, wherein I could possibly, in any respect have done better.

✠ Resolved, Never to give over, nor in the least to slacken, my fight with my corruptions, however unsuccessful I may be.

✠ Resolved, After afflictions, to inquire, what I am the better for them; what good I have got by them; and, what I might have got by them.

✠ Resolved, Always to do that, which I shall wish I had done when I see others do it.

✠ Let there be something of benevolence in all that I speak.

April 1991

**The York family. Front row, left to right: Betsy Ross, Sgt. Alvin C. York, in his lap Mary Alice; wife Miss Gracie, in her lap Thomas Jefferson. Back row, left to right; Woodrow Wilson, Alvin Jr., Andrew Jackson.**

# SERGEANT YORK
## LAST OF THE LONG HUNTERS

∽ BY ∽

## TOM SKEYHILL
OFFICIAL BIOGRAPHER OF
SERGEANT ALVIN C. YORK

*ILLUSTRATED*

Published by:         Larry Harrison
Christian Book Gallery
9066 Knickerbocker
St. John, Indiana 46373

*Printed by*
**Bible & Literature Missionary Foundation**
713 Cannon Boulevard
Shelbyville, Tennessee 37160

TO

# THE YORK BOYS

ALVIN, JR.
GEORGE EDWARD BUXTON
WOODROW WILSON
SAM HOUSTON
ANDREW JACKSON

# THE WHITE HOUSE
**WASHINGTON**

May 28, 1930

Sgt. Alvin C. York,
President, The Alvin C. York
Agricultural Institute,
Jamestown, Tennessee.

My dear Sergeant York:

The work you are doing to carry
the light of knowledge to boys and
girls is part of a movement for uni-
versal education that has been an un-
denied passion of our country and
therefore cannot fail to attract the
warmest sympathy of all our people. I
wish you full success in your en-
deavors.

Yours faithfully,

Herbert Hoover

# Contents

# Author's Note

The author wishes to acknowledge his indebtedness to the officers of the War Department, in Washington, D. C., and to Colonel George Edward Buxton, Providence, Rhode Island, for permitting him to examine and copy all of their documents connected with the York episode; to Captain E. C. B. Danforth, Jr., and Sergeant Harry Parsons for their assistance in helping him document the story; to Mr. Charles J. Strahan, Deputy-Assistant Commissioner of Education for New Jersey; Mr. Howard Dare White, Assistant Commissioner of Education for New Jersey; Mr. John Spargo, Assistant Commissioner of Education for New Jersey; Mr. William A. Ackerman, Chief of Bureau of Academic Credentials, Director of State Summer Schools and Teachers Institute for New Jersey; Mr. E. T. Cameron, Executive Secretary of the Michigan Education Association; Dr. Harlan H. Horner, Executive Secretary, New York State Teachers Association; Mr. F. L. Pinet, Executive Secretary of the Kansas State Teachers Association; Mr. E. L. Miller, Assistant Superintendent of Schools, Detroit, Michigan; Mr. Claud S. Lazelere, of the History Department, Central State Teachers College in Michigan; and Principal W. N. Van Slyke, Topeka High School, Topeka, Kansas, for their great help in going over the completed manuscript.

To Mrs. Matthew Page Gaffney, of the Great Neck High School, Great Neck, New York, for her fine work in checking the vocabulary and the entire story. To Mrs. John Trotwood Moore, State Librarian and Historian, Nashville, Tennessee; Mr. Meriwether Lewis, head of the Reference Department of Carnegie Library, Nashville, Tennessee; and to Major Oscar L. Farris, Nashville, Tennessee, for generously supplying the author with innumerable reference books. To Miss Agnes Selley, of Nashville, Tennessee, for typing the manuscript and checking all documents. To Mr. A. S. Bushing and Mr. Garrett, respectively secretary and legal adviser to Sergeant Alvin C. York; the members of the York family; Pastor Pile; and to the hundreds of other mountaineers who by their willingness to coöperate with the author during his frequent visits to the mountains helped to make the story possible.

Without the loyal and gracious help of all of these, he could not have written the story of America's most distinguished soldier. He, therefore, gratefully acknowledges and appreciates all they have done for him and through him for Sergeant Alvin C. York.

# SERGEANT YORK
## LAST OF THE LONG HUNTERS

## CHAPTER I

## America's One-Man Army

RED dawn in the Argonne. A thin brown line of doughboys is crouching under the parapet, eagerly awaiting the whistle blast which is to send them over the top, out across No Man's Land, and through the German trenches a mile away. They have been up all night and are tired and cold. Their pockets are bulging with grenades. Their bayonets are fixed. This is to be an attack with the cold steel.

The forest reverberates with all the hideous and deafening sounds of war: the staccato bark of machine guns, the crash of bombs, the whine of bullets, and the scream and roar of the big shells high overhead. The air is slightly tainted with the odor of rotten pears, which means the gas—the deadly gas—which bursts the lungs, tears out the throat, and topples men over, writhing and sobbing, until death ends their agony.   The word is passed quickly from mouth to mouth along the line— "Gas masks!"

Over on the right, eyes glued to his watch, crouches the captain, a gallant young Southerner.   He has studied his instructions very carefully and knows that this is to be a general attack.   Tens of thousands of doughboys for miles up and down the line, in a few seconds, are going over the top.   Zero, the attacking time, is set for 6.10 A. M.   It is almost that now. The captain is going to take his company over in two waves, with about one hundred men in each.   He is going to lead the first wave himself, and his junior officer, Lieutenant Stewart of Alabama, is to lead the second.

Over on the left, with one foot on the fire ledge and his head just under the parapet, crouches a tall, red-headed, raw-boned Tennessee mountaineer.   Back home in the mountains he is known as the greatest shot that ever squinted down the long barrel of a muzzle-loader and "busted" a turkey's head.   The purest Anglo-Saxon blood in the world flows in his veins, and his dialect is similar to the language which Chaucer and Shakespeare used hundreds of years ago. Rumor has it that he was several times a conscientious objector before going to camp. This morning he is destined to fight probably the greatest individual fight in the annals of modern or legendary warfare. He is going over in the second wave.

Suddenly a shrill whistle blast rises above the other sounds of battle. The gallant captain hurls himself over the top, and, followed by a hundred doughboys, starts down the hillside and out across No Man's Land toward the German trenches. Although they know that they are going to almost certain death, they advance as coolly and steadily as if they were merely maneuvering back home in their old training camp.

Suddenly, when they are halfway across, hell breaks loose. A number of German machine guns hidden in the brush on the hillside over on the left front lay a machine-gun barrage in front of them. The air is soon a driving sleet of splintered lead, and the doughboys go down like ripe corn before the reaper's blade.   Some utter little whimpering cries of pain and pitch forward on their faces.   Others stop suddenly in their stride, clutch desperately at a wounded arm or leg, and fall.   Yet others gasp, draw in their breath with a sucking sound, stagger forward a few yards, and collapse.

Only seventeen, including the leader, get through that terrible wall of death. Knowing that he cannot hope to accomplish anything with such a small handful, he orders them to tumble into shell craters, tumbles into one himself, and whistles and motions for the second wave to hurry up.

The Germans lengthen their range.

Lieutenant Stewart, several yards out in front of his men, falls with a bullet above the knee, twists and rolls over with excruciating pain, and then gallantly arises and, dragging a game leg, carries on.   Another bullet shatters his elbow.   And still he carries on.   A third bullet crashes between the eyes and puts an end to his agony forever.

Sergeant Harry Parsons, a vaudeville actor from Brooklyn, New York, takes charge.   He has seen the first wave almost entirely wiped out. He sees his own men falling all around him. He sums up the situation. Before the second wave has been massacred, he very wisely orders them to tumble into shell craters while he reconnoiters.

The attack is stopped in its tracks. But it must not be. The company must keep up with the general advance. The Americans must get up and at all costs carry the German positions. They must! But it is impossible. At least it is impossible until the terrible machine-gun fire is stopped.

Parsons sweeps the surrounding country with his glasses and locates nearly thirty machine guns screened in the brush on the hillside over on the left front, deep in German territory. As a trained soldier he knows that machine guns fire up to one thousand shots a minute, that bullets come out of their muzzles almost as continuously as water out of a hose, and that German machine gunners can trace their initials with bullets on sandbags. These particular machine gunners are firing from a dominating height in broad daylight into open country. Over twenty thousand shots a minute are pouring down upon the battle field, kicking up the dust, ripping holes in the ground, and forcing the doughboys to keep their heads well under the level of the shell craters.

A thousand men with bayonets and bombs in a frontal attack could not hope to attack thirty machine gunners successfully. Five thousand men could not; nor ten thousand—not in a frontal attack in broad daylight. The sergeant most certainly has not ten thousand men. He has not ten hundred—not one hundred. Nevertheless he must knock out the machine guns, rally his men, and press home the attack. He considers the situation carefully and then orders seventeen doughboys to drop back, deploy to the left, go out across No Man's Land, through the German lines, and get the machine gunners. Madness! Suicide! A million-to-one chance! Just the same he issues the order. To the everlasting credit of the doughboys, let it be said that, although they knew they were going to certain death, they whooped with joy and maneuvered to execute the command.

Sergeant Alvin C. York, America's One-Man Army

The "Detail of Death," for such it really turned out to be, was made up of three squads with a corporal in charge of each, and Sergeant Bernard Early commanding the whole.

The seventeen of them crawled back a few yards and moved over slightly to the left. Sergeant Early then called the big red-headed mountaineer. "You are a woodsman and a hunter," he said. "Lead us to those machine guns."

The big fellow answered with only two words, in the language of his people, "Right smart!" and took the lead.

All his life he had hunted red and gray fox, stalked deer and wild turkey, and slipped noiselessly through the forest after the chattering squirrel. He knew, as few men know, the value of stealth, cover, and quickness. Quietly and swiftly he led the doughboys through the brush, from tree to tree, around the bases of hills, always keeping his followers in the shadows or under cover. He led them out across No Man's Land and through the enemy lines without the Germans even seeing or firing a shot at them.

In single file, with their rifles and bayonets in their hands, they penetrated deeper and deeper into German territory. Suddenly, somewhere behind the German lines and over a mile ahead of the American advance, they "flushed" two enemy stretcher bearers coming down the forest trail toward them. Immediately upon sighting them the Germans turned around and dashed madly back through the trees whence they had come. The doughboys at once gave chase. Some of them leveled their rifles to fire.

The mountaineer's hunting habits again asserted themselves. "Don't fire," he shouted. "We will trail them to their dens, and then we will know where their dens are." He knew that the red and gray foxes circle and generally come back. He figured that the two Germans would instinctively return to the machine-gun battalion—not in front of it to be killed by their own fire, but behind it—exactly where he wanted to lead the doughboys.

Deeper and deeper into the forest they penetrated—two hundred yards—three hundred yards—four hundred. Suddenly the two terrified Germans swung sharply to the right, broke through the trees, and disappeared. The doughboys, right on top of them, smashed through the forest, jumped across a small stream, and, to their amazement, landed almost on top of the headquarters staff of the machine-gun battalion.

It was a complete surprise on both sides. Five German officers, in shirt sleeves, were standing up examining a map; thirty noncommissioned officers were sitting around a chow can; and stretcher bearers, runners, orderlies, and privates were lying around smoking, eating, and talking. Coffee was steaming in a big pot, and jams, jellies, bread, and meat were all over the place. They had been quietly breakfasting in the early morning, behind their own lines in absolute security—so they thought—when suddenly, out of the forest, yelling like red Indians, and charging with the cold steel, came the doughboys. The Germans, thunderstruck, panic-stricken, naturally thought that the line had broken and the whole Allied army was on top of them. They threw up their hands and surrendered without firing a shot.

The doughboys were just as surprised, but they were the quicker thinkers and carried through the bluff.

Sergeant Early reassumed command. "We've got them!  We've got them!  Line them up in columns of two, keep their hands up, and let's get them out quick," he shouted.

The big mountaineer was not quite so confident.  His hunting habits had trained him to be always on the alert and to expect the unexpected.  He never relaxed, even for a fraction of a second.  With his hand on the butt of his pistol, he moved a few paces ahead, scouting.

Suddenly one of the captured officers called out a command in German.  The doughboys, not understanding, simply turned and told him to shut up.  In the same instant the prisoners threw themselves flat on their faces, and German machine guns screened in the brush on the hillside a few yards away vomited and spewed flaming hell in the faces of the Americans. Literally speaking they were caught "flat-footed."  The sergeant gasped with pain, spat out a mouthful of blood, and went

down with several bullets in his body. One
corporal fell riddled by over two hundred
bullets—he never knew what hit him.
Another had an "X" shot in his helmet;
every button was cut from his uniform and
he was hit in the arm and side. Six of the
privates were either wounded or killed in
that sudden and terrible blast of death.

Only seven privates and a corporal
remained unhurt. Two of the privates
jumped behind a big tree, three hurled
themselves into the brush, and two flopped
down behind the prisoners, held them, and
saved their own lives. One and only one
stood his ground—Corporal Alvin York.

Mountaineers are suspicious, and hunters,
as I have said, are trained to be on the
alert. He was a rare combination of both.
When the German officers issued the command, he wheeled around like a flash and,
knowing that there was something wrong,
dived for the ground. Bullets whanged
through his canteen, grazed his shrapnel
helmet, plowed up the ground at his feet,
and tore a tunnel through the undergrowth
behind him. Miraculously, not one of
them hit him. His situation, however, was

desperate, to say the least. The prisoners behind were likely to jump him at any moment. Unquestionably, enemy soldiers lurked in the woods on both sides and in front. Up on the hillside machine guns were spitting almost certain death right in his face. Any other man would have been lost because any other man's mind would have been filled with so many conflicting ideas and emotions that he would have been momentarily paralyzed and killed. "Shall I fight?" "Shall I run?" "Shall I stay here?" "Shall I crawl away?" "Shall I surrender?" These and a thousand other awful thoughts would have rushed through the mind of any ordinary man. Mountaineers are not ordinary men. They think one thought at a time, and they think that thought through. The big red-headed corporal had only one thought in his mind. He had gone to war to fight. He had gone after the machine gunners to fight them. All right! He would fight them. He was a deeply religious man and was firmly convinced that so long as he believed in God no harm could befall him. Besides, he was one of the greatest shots in the world, and the distance, twenty-five yards, was his favorite shooting distance.

The first thing he did was to apply a favorite motto of his mother's, "When you are in danger, slow up and think fast." He slowed up and thought fast. Next he made himself comfortable, swung his shoulders around, loosened up his clothing, hitched his pistol holster around so that he could get at it if he was rushed, and then, because he liked to shoot offhand, suddenly stood up, covered the machine gunners, and shot them up with as extraordinary an exhibition of rapid, daring, and accurate shooting as the world has ever known. He fired eighteen times, hit eighteen Germans squarely between the eyes, and forced the survivors, confused and shaken, to take cover.

Later, when questioned by General Pershing, he explained how easy it is to shoot up a German machine-gun battalion. Easy, that is, if you know how. "Every time I seed a German I jes' teched him off." He supplemented this simple statement with the even simpler one that in order to shoot him the Germans had to see him; that in order to see him they had to put up their heads.  And he added, "I had to put their heads down again."

After this terrific and terrible attack, delivered with the swiftness and accuracy of a dead shot, the firing slackened and he was master of the situation.  He glanced back over his shoulder.  The two dough-boys were holding the prisoners.  He glanced swiftly to both sides.  Barely in time.  Six German soldiers and an officer crouching in a gun pit only twenty yards away, summing up the situation and realiz-ing that they had only one man to deal with, suddenly leaped to their feet and rushed him with the naked steel.  He dropped his rifle, flipped out his pistol, and achieved what was probably the outstand-ing individual feat of the war.  He shot the seventh German first—then the sixth— then the fifth—and so on, killing the leader, the officer, last.  The fallen bodies over-lapped in a straight line.  Later, when asked why he shot the rear ones first, he explained that when hunting turkey in the mountains of Tennessee, he always shot the rear ones first, in order that the front

The cave on the mountain side, in the Valley of the Three Forks of the Wolf, where the Long Hunter lived nearly one hundred fifty years ago

ones, thinking that he was missing, would keep coming. Grimly he commented, "Had I have shot the leaders, the rear ones would have abandoned the rush, dropped down under cover, and later sniped me from the rear."

Cautiously another German head appeared over the top of the trench and several bursts of machine-gun bullets kicked up the dust around his feet. He "teched" him off too. The commanding officer, a prisoner, witnessing this shooting and realizing that the mountaineer would most certainly kill them all unless something was done, wriggled over and inquired, "What are you?"

At this psychological moment another German head appeared. The big fellow's rifle barked. The score was now twenty-seven.

The major continued, "Are you English?" When the mountaineer answered, "No; American," he dropped on his knees in astonishment and assured the "one-man army" that if he agreed not to kill any more he would make them surrender.

"Can you?" grimly inquired the corporal.

That touched the Prussian officer's vanity. He leaped to his feet, clipped his heels together, and arrogantly answered, "I am their commanding officer. If I blow this whistle, of course they will surrender."

That was enough for the mountaineer. Panther-like he sprang at the officer, pushed his pistol between his eyes, and ordered, "Blow that thar whistle and blow it right smart!"

The officer blew it, the firing ceased instantly, and the German machine gunners came out of the trenches with their hands up. The impossible, the incredible, the unbelievable, the outstanding individual feat of the war was consummated.

In their own territory, in broad daylight, and in fair fight, a German machine-gun battalion had been whipped and captured by one brave and gallant American doughboy.

## Chapter II

# The Long Hunters

SERGEANT YORK'S life story is one of the greatest stories in the world today. It is stranger than fiction, stranger than life itself, and just as intangible. Edgar Allan Poe nor H. G. Wells nor Dumas would have dared to create such a character, and had one of them done so he would have seemed incredible. People would say that such a man could not have lived. But Alvin York did live and lives today.

His story rightly begins back in the closing years of the eighteenth century—in the time of Daniel Boone.

Over a hundred fifty years ago, the whole country was thrilling to the great discoveries of that intrepid hunter, fighter, explorer, and pioneer of pioneers. Throughout the cities, towns, and villages of the East, the news was passing that Boone had broken through the mountains and blazed

(17)

a trail to what is now called Kentucky. Marvelous stories were circulated of the richness of the soil, abundance of wild game, and potential wealth of this new country, which, on account of the savage Indian fights, was soon to be known as the Dark and Bloody Ground.

Adventurous, pioneering, land-hungry men and women turned their eyes westward. Expedition after expedition was organized and sent out to seek what was hoped would be a land of milk and honey.

The most famous of all these expeditions was that of the Long Hunters. Over forty of the most successful hunters of New River and Holston Valley organized a company and obtained a charter to hunt and trap west of the Cumberland Mountains. Under their leaders, Joseph Drake and Henry Skaggs—two of the best hunters and woodsmen in the mountains—they set out in the fall of 1770. Each hunter was equipped with three pack horses, rifles, ammunition, dogs, and salt. They all wore tasseled and fringed deerskin shirts, belts bristling with knives and tomahawks, coonskin caps with the tails hanging down

their shoulders, and soft buffalo-hide moccasins. They were away for a long
time. Their rifles were those wonderful
old smooth-barreled, long muzzle-loaders.
Hence the name "Long Hunters."

They pushed through the Gap and,
traveling fast, soon reached Kentucky.
From the top of the hill at Knoblocks,
overlooking the widest and deepest salt
licks they had ever seen, they saw what
they estimated at "largely over one thousand animals, including buffalo, elk, bear,
and deer, with many wild turkeys scattered about them. All were quite restless,
some playing and others busily licking the
earth. At length they took flight and
bounded away all in one direction, so that
in a brief space of a couple of minutes
not an animal was to be seen."

Throughout most of the winter the Long
Hunters successfully trapped, hunted, and
explored, and before spring had collected a
large shipment of skins, furs, and smoked
meat, which, shortly afterwards, during
their absence from camp, was stolen by the
Cherokees. Nothing daunted, they continued their hunting along the Green and

Cumberland rivers, and so abundant was the game that in an incredibly short time they had replaced their loss with an even more valuable collection.

One night a party of Long Hunters were hunting along the Green River when to their astonishment they heard the words of an old English ballad floating through the trees. Pushing through the forest, they discovered a splendidly built white man lying on his back singing to his heart's content. It was Daniel Boone.

The Long Hunters were away from home for over eleven months, and their hunt is still regarded as one of the most picturesque and successful in the history of the mountain country. One of them, a lean, tall, red-headed young man named Coonrod Pile, had left a girl behind him. Away out there in Kentucky, hunting, fighting, and pioneering, he never ceased to think of her. After the hunt was over, he set out, a few days ahead of his companions, to rejoin her.

Kentucky was a wilderness at that time. The Indians were "bad medicine." There were practically no trails, no bridges across the streams, and no stop-over places—

nothing like that.   The threat of starvation, exposure, being lost in the wilderness, of losing one's scalp or worse than that—of the terrible torture and death by the "slow fire," were ever present.

Coonrod Pile laid in a supply of salt, filled his powderhorn and soft doeskin pouch with powder and shot, sharpened his tomahawk and hunting knife, slung his long, smooth-bored rifle across his shoulder and headed back for Virginia and the girl. We can easily picture him, dressed in his hunter's costume, pushing on and on through the forest, hunting and killing his meat, carefully concealing ·his camp fire at night, and fighting off or evading the Indians.

While traveling across the shoulder of what is now called middle-eastern Tennessee, he came upon a little valley in the heart of the mountains.   It was watered with bubbling springs and sparkling streams, vividly green, teeming with game and surrounded by blue mountains.   On the banks of the river which ran through the valley he shot a wolf, and after the manner of the pioneers called it Wolf River.   Because

Wolf River split into three forks at the entrance to the little valley, he named it "The Valley of the Three Forks of the Wolf." That was nearly a century and a half ago, and it has the same name today. The Long Hunter remained there for several days, sleeping at night in a cave on the mountain side. The very first morning a deer came to drink at the mouth of a near-by spring. He had venison for breakfast.

Coonrod Pile returned to Virginia, married the girl of his choice, and brought her back to the little valley. They were the first white people to settle there.

He built a log cabin, plowed the ground with a scooter plow, raised a large family, prospered exceedingly, and soon was the richest and most powerful man in all that part of the mountains. Two of his sons were killed by the bushwhackers in the Civil War. A grandson was wounded on the heights of Chapultepec in Mexico.

A few years before the World War, William York, Alvin's father, was living in the valley. He was born in the cabin of the Long Hunter and blacksmithed in the original cave of the Long Hunter on the

mountain side. He blacksmithed by day
and hunted coon and possum by night.
He was a mighty hunter, a dead shot, and
a man of great moral character. He used
to shoe mules—and, according to his
famous son, he never "backed up on a
mule" in his life, but would always stand
his ground regardless of danger from the
many vicious hoofs. This shows moral
character. One day a mean mule "lashed
out and connected," and shortly afterwards
the blacksmith died of typhoid fever—no
mountaineer would ever admit that he died
from a mule kick. That left his wife with
eleven children, most of them red-headed,
to bring up all alone in a one-room log
cabin on the mountain side fifty miles from
the nearest railroad. Alvin was the third
son and the great-great-grandson of the
Long Hunter.

During the hundred fifty years which
elapsed between the coming of the Long
Hunter and the death of the blacksmith,
the mountains were invaded and settled by
the liberty-loving, God-fearing, resourceful,
red-headed, raw-boned, and "gangling"
Scotch-Irish.

The term Scotch-Irish is misleading. They were neither Scotch nor Irish. They were the purest Anglo-Saxons in the world. Centuries ago England used them as a buffer against Scotland and later sent them over to Ireland to help colonize that turbulent but beautiful country. Hence the name Scotch-Irish.

Despairing of finding either religious or political freedom in the old country, they crossed the seas and came over here, where they hoped to find freedom from political oppression and the right to worship God according to the dictates of their own consciences. They followed the Quakers into Pennsylvania. However, they were ever a restless brood. If a Scotch-Irishman built a log cabin in the wilderness and then heard that another settler had built within fifty miles of him, he felt crowded and moved.

Over one hundred years ago they left Pennsylvania and trekked down the Shenandoah Valley, slipped through the mountains, and settled on the Yadkin in North Carolina. Later they broke through the barrier of the Great Smokies, swept across the Tennessee Valley, pioneered the Cumberlands, and continued across the Dark and Bloody Ground as far west as the Ozarks.

They were mighty fighters. Outnumbered, they went up King's Mountain like a tornado and whipped Ferguson and his redcoats in one of the turning battles of the Revolutionary War. They followed Old Hickory to New Orleans and, again outnumbered, annihilated the flower of Wellington's continental army, an army that was regarded as the finest in the world. Yet the Scotch-Irish, under their beloved leader, made short work of it. They were equally effective against the red men. They whipped the Creeks and the Cherokees in many decisive battles, and forced them either to live in peace or to move farther west. When they were not fighting redcoats or redskins, they were fighting nature. They blasted their farms out of the mountain side. They broke trails where there had never been trails before. They reached forth their hands and tamed the wilderness.

They were God-fearing men and women— no rituals or liturgy for them, no prayer books.   Their God was the God of the Old Testament, stern but just.   They permitted nothing to stand between them and their God but the Bible.

They were liberty-loving.   That is why they had come to America.   Here they fought, bled, and died for liberty; achieved and clung tenaciously to it.   They would endure no political bosses, no partisan dictatorship.

Probably no more resourceful men and women ever lived.   Every man was his own gunsmith, carpenter, hunter, cobbler, farmer, and everything else.   And the women!   Those wonderful pioneer women, in their linsey dresses and split bonnets, were equally resourceful; carding, weaving, spinning, cooking, dressmaking, and raising large families.

They founded an empire within this republic — the empire of "Appalachia," which is the term by which the mountaineers describe the mountainous parts of North Carolina, West Virginia, Tennessee, and Kentucky.

# CHAPTER III

## Redcoats

WHEN the Revolutionary War broke out, and the English king, through his redcoats, reached across the seas and threatened the liberty of the Colonists, the mountaineers rose in their might and at King's Mountain scattered his armies like chaff before the wind.

The importance of their victory on these crag-crowned slopes cannot possibly be overestimated. It marked the turning point in the battles of the Revolutionary War. The cause of the Colonists in 1780 seemed lost. Even Washington was discouraged and admitted that he had practically lost all hope. Charleston had fallen. General Gates had been defeated, and Sumter was having a hard time. Lord Cornwallis had just been reinforced by three thousand men, and with banners waving and trumpets blowing was marching into North Carolina.

In the mountain states Ferguson and his redcoats were sweeping everything before them and devastating far and wide. "Tell that set of banditti," he wrote to Shelby, "to stay at home and keep quiet, or I will cross the mountains and have their hornet's nest burned out." On another occasion he referred to the mountaineers as "those barbarians from the backwoods."

The mountaineers met the challenge. They had traveled thousands of miles in search of liberty; and had found it after untold sacrifices, cold, hunger, starvation, Indian fights, and all the other hardships of those early pioneer days. While there was a drop of red blood left in their veins, they were grimly determined not to give it up to any English king or redcoat. If Ferguson insisted on regarding them as banditti and backwoods barbarians, so much the worse for him.

Throughout the mountains, from the Great Smokies to the Cumberlands, the call went out for volunteers to thrash this arrogant redcoat. The response was instantaneous. From the coves and the back creeks, from the mountain hamlets and the river settlements, all who could walk or ride "toted" their old-fashioned muzzle-loaders and poured into camp at Watauga Old Fields, which was the rendezvous of the border troops. They had not a single bayonet among them. They carried neither bedding nor tents. They killed their own meat. Their uniform was the rough garb of the pioneer—homespun hunting shirt and leggings, fringed and tasseled, and coonskin or mink cap, with the tail hanging down. But they were the most expert marksmen in the world. They had to be, or they would never have been able to resist the Indians successfully and supply themselves and their families with deer, bear, and buffalo meat. A number of them came directly from a turkey shoot, where they had been "busting" gobblers' heads with their flintlock rifles from a distance of sixty yards.

The leaders, too, were pioneers and men of heroic stature. Campbell, Shelby, and Sevier were names to conjure with in the history of the backwoods.

John Sevier, who was to be the first governor of Tennessee, was the most dashing and picturesque of them all.  A fearless fighter, he also possessed those qualities of statesmanship which marked the empire builder.  His name and the story of his deeds were known and revered in almost every mountain cabin.  Handsome and fearless, he was as well fitted to be the hero of romance as to be the leader of the Watauga settlement.  He had participated in innumerable sieges and Indian fights and had always emerged victorious.

On one memorable occasion the little community in which he was one of the leaders was surprised by the redskins.  Men, women, and children were hurriedly collected in the fort, the heavy gates of which were slammed and barred in the faces of the foremost savages.  Some women, milking, were left outside.  Sevier insisted that the gates be opened to allow a number of young men, led by himself, to effect the rescue.  The older and wiser men demurred on the ground that it would not be right to jeopardize the safety of all in order to save the lives of two or three young women.  All deplored the situation, and there was not a man present who would not willingly have risked death to save the milkers, but they had to think of the many before the few. The women and children in the fort came first.

The gates were not opened. At a signal from the garrison the young women dashed for the safety of the walls. One of them, Kate Sherrill, the youngest and most beautiful girl in the community, was headed off by the savage and war-mad Indians. Running swiftly, she dodged and doubled while her companions reached the outside of the fort, where they were quickly seized by strong and friendly hands and lifted and pulled into safety. By this time, Kate was almost exhausted. The Indians were rapidly closing in on her. Sevier could stand it no longer. Rifle and tomahawk in hand, he leaped over the stockade, momentarily scattered the redskins, and rescued the beautiful and by now almost hysterical girl. "Bonny Kate," as she was called, later married her dashing young rescuer.

The mountaineers, with the swift daring of their kind, decided not to wait for Ferguson and his redcoats, but to carry the battle to them, and if possible effect a surprise attack. The English commander with 1,125 men was camped on the top of King's Mountain, where he was confident that he could not be beaten. He had thrown up breastworks of earth and stone, behind which were his tents and baggage wagons, with glint of steel and flash of scarlet uniforms, and the Union Jack of England flying over all.

What chance had these English redcoats against these tall, rangy mountaineers who knew the forests and the mountains as well as the squirrels and the bears knew them, and who could shoot straighter and reload more quickly than men had ever done before? Nine hundred strong they set out for the mountains to prove to Colonel Patrick Ferguson of the 71st Regiment of the British Infantry that if they were hornets they at least had not lost their sting. Silently and swiftly they stole through the trees and up the slate ridges, determined not to waste a bullet nor to shoot until they saw the whites of the enemies' eyes. Colonel Ferguson jeered and continued to call them "banditti." The

redcoats futilely fired volley after volley
down the mountain side at them. Grimly,
resolutely, taking advantage of the under-
brush and holding their fire, the mountaineers pressed on and up; and when they
knew they could not miss, they calmly
leveled their long muzzle-loaders and picked
off the amazed English soldiers.

The British were brave enough, but they
had never faced fire like this before. They
did not even know there were such marksmen in the world. Useless, they thought,
to match shots with them; better to use
the cold steel. They fixed bayonets and
with cheers charged down the mountain
side. But the stings of the hornets choked
the cheers in their throats and forced them
back in disorder. The mountaineers pressed
on and up, firing as they climbed. Confusion and panic seized the redcoats. Ferguson, on horseback, tried to escape. One of
the Watauga "backwoods banditti" sighted
along his rifle, gently pulled the trigger,
and the fiery English colonel who had
despised the purest Anglo-Saxon stock in
the world, pitched from his saddle with a
bullet through the heart. The British lost

over four hundred killed and wounded and about seven hundred prisoners. The Americans lost, in wounded and killed, only eighty-eight.

"The victory," says Theodore Roosevelt, "was of far-reaching importance and ranks among the decisive battles of the Revolution. It was the first great success of the Americans in the South, the turning point in the Southern campaign, and it brought cheer to the patriots throughout the Union."

More than that, it demonstrated to the young nation that these mountaineers in homespun shirts and coonskin caps, with their old flintlock rifles, were fitted to match blows with any soldiers in the world. If they could ever be trained, equipped, and led by inspired leaders, they would be a force to be reckoned with.

As fate would have it, they found this inspired leadership in Andrew Jackson, and under his command at New Orleans in the War of 1812, they again proved their fighting worth.

"Old Hickory" possessed military genius of a high order and was a born leader of men. He was a strict disciplinarian and

had hanged and shot soldiers for infringe-
ment of military discipline. He knew the
mountaineers as few men know them—
their ability to endure hardships, their
unfailing courage under fire, their deadly
skill with the rifle, and their burning
patriotism. The greater part of his troops
were recruited from the mountains of
Tennessee and Kentucky. Campaigning
against the Creeks and later against the
Spaniards at Pensacola, he had molded
them into a first-class army, bending them
to his discipline and training them to fight
under unified command.

He was distinctly the fighting type of
general and preferred to lead his men from
the front and not from the rear. He was
always in the thick of the fight and had had
many narrow escapes from a soldier's death.
He was one of the most pugnacious fighters
that ever lived. He was the killer type.
Chivalrous almost to a fault, loyal and loving toward his friends, he nevertheless was
harder than hickory the moment he was in
a fight.

His duel with Dickinson reveals the iron
courage and the grim determination of this

extraordinary pioneer fighter and statesman.  Dickinson, who was one of the greatest shots and most expert duelists in the
country, had declared publicly that Major
General Andrew Jackson was a worthless
scoundrel, a poltroon, and coward.  "Old
Hickory," although he was not by any
means a great shot, and had had no experience in dueling, immediately challenged his
attacker.  Their seconds arranged everything:

It is agreed that the distance shall be twenty-four
feet; the parties to stand facing each other, their
pistols down perpendicularly.  When they are
ready, the single word, "Fire," to be given; at
which they are to fire as soon as they please.  Should
either fire before the word is given, we pledge out-
selves to shoot him down instantly.  The person
to give the word to be determined by lot, as also
the choice of position.  We mutually agree that the
above regulations shall be observed in the affair of
honor depending between General Andrew Jackson
and Charles Dickinson, Esq.

Everyone believed that Dickinson was
sure to win; and he himself was so confident
that he offered to bet five hundred dollars
he would drop his opponent with the first

shot. Jackson—and this shows the stuff of which "Old Hickory" was made—had secretly decided to let his opponent fire first. He felt reasonably sure that Dickinson would hit him, and he made up his mind to take the ball.

"I shall hit him even if he shoots me through the brain," he said to Overton, his second.

In the rising dawn of a beautiful May morning they faced each other—Jackson, tall, thin, with a great crop of tousled hair just turning gray, wore a long coat which was loosely folded in order to deceive Dickinson, who most certainly would fire straight for his heart. Dickinson was smiling, confident, and debonair. At the word, "Fire," he raised his right arm with the speed of lightning and pulled the trigger. Jackson clutched at his left breast but did not fall. His face was a mask and his eyes, cold and hard, looked straight ahead at his opponent. With the exception of the involuntary movement of the hand, he made no move or sign to show whether he had been hit or not. Slowly and deliberately he raised his pistol. Dickinson's smile of triumph turned to astonishment and then to fear.

"Great God, have I missed him?" he moaned, and moved slightly away from the mark, whereupon Overton pointed his pistol at him and ordered him back.

The doomed man regained control of himself and stood waiting. Andrew Jackson took his time, sighted carefully, and pressed the trigger. Dickinson fell dying, with a bullet through the body. When Jackson calmly and steadily walked over to the seconds, they observed that his shoes were full of blood.

"Are you hit?" inquired Overton.

"Oh, I believe he pinked me a little," Jackson answered. Dickinson's bullet had just missed his heart, breaking two ribs and raking his breastbone.

This was the sort of man who led the mountaineers from victory to victory until the power of both the redskins and the redcoats in the South was broken forever.

In December, 1814, a large British force under General Edward Pakenham, crossed the seas and anchored off New Orleans. Obviously they intended to capture the

Andrew Jackson took his time, sighted carefully, and pressed the trigger

unprotected city. There were fourteen thousand of them, mostly old soldiers, veterans of many hard-fought battles on the other side, and the flower of Wellington's continental army. They must have been secretly amused when they heard that a backwoods general contemplated leading twenty-five hundred squirrel hunters against them.

The whole United States was worried. The odds were too great. Disaster was regarded as almost certain by everybody except Old Hickory and his men. Arriving in the vicinity of New Orleans, they threw up earthen breastworks. Old Hickory armed his men with spades and machetes and ordered them to dig night and day. When they murmured against his slave-driving tactics and remonstrated that they had come to fight and not to dig, he threatened to have them hanged or shot as traitors if they said another word.

On the morning of the historic battle, he and his men were well under cover and invisible to the enemy. They stood three and four deep behind the breastworks, so that the moment a man fired he could step back and reload while another took his place. Thus a continuous firing was maintained. Again the backwoods order was delivered, "Don't shoot until you see the whites of their eyes." The cannons were placed with equal skill.

At dawn on the morning of January 8, 1815, Congreve rockets soared up from the British lines, and the next moment the battle began. The veterans of continental wars with bands playing, bayonets flashing, and visions in their minds of being in New Orleans that night, marched to the attack in massed formation. Scotch highlanders marched with Irish fusilladers, grenadiers, and bombardiers. Plumes were waving. Uniforms streaked the mist with red. Rockets flamed overhead and on all sides. From rear and flank came the belching and roaring of English cannons. The mountaineers held their fire. The redcoats were only three hundred yards away now; and yet behind the breastworks not a man was to be seen. Not a trigger was touched. Not a fuse was lighted. The greatest shots in the world were waiting until they were sure of their targets.

Suddenly, as the redcoats pressed forward within two hundred yards of the defenders, a flash of lightning, a crash of thunder, and a cloud of acrid battle smoke came from the American lines. The British front ranks stopped as if they had run up against a concrete wall. Hundreds fell in that first awful volley, in which practically every bullet had found its mark. This was quite different from what the attackers had expected. Never had they encountered such terrible, accurate, and continuous fire. As volley followed volley, their lines wavered and fell back. Pakenham, twice wounded and trying to rally them, was shot dead. Other high-ranking officers were singled out and deliberately picked off by these mountain marksmen. The American cannons, too, fired with equal effect, ripped great lanes through the attacking forces, crushed them, and hurled them back in confusion.

No soldiers in the world could stand up against that sort of fire.

The British veterans fell back panic-stricken and defeated, leaving over forty-five hundred wounded and dead on the battle field.    Only twenty-one Americans were injured.

Out on the high seas a frail little ship was bending her broad white sails in all haste toward the port of New Orleans, with the news that fifteen days before, in Ghent, Belgium, peace between England and the United States had been declared.    The hideous slaughter had been in vain.    These gallant English lads had given their lives in a useless battle which would never have been allowed to occur in modern times, when news of a treaty is immediately broadcast by radio and rushed by telephone, telegraph, and cable to all the countries of the world.

Old Hickory and his brave mountaineers had fought a desperate fight which had seemed necessary for their freedom, but native in their hearts was the peace of the dim forests from which they had come and this useless slaughter was not to their liking.

## Chapter IV

# Redskins

OVER one hundred years ago, the mountains were a hunter's paradise, with mighty herds of buffalo, deer, and elk roaming through the valleys and over the hills, and bears, wolves, panthers, bobcats, foxes, and other wild beasts frequenting the forests and the canebrakes. These animals at regular intervals visited the salt licks which were formed from the saline deposits of sulphur springs, and in the course of years often licked great furrows several feet deep for long distances in the ground.

The Indians, knowing this, visited these licks, hunting and killing. The white settlers quickly found this out and began building their forts and stockades near by. Clashes with the redskins, who regarded these hunting grounds as their own, were inevitable. Blood was spilled, reprisals made, and the fires of hatred fanned. The settlers, believing that the only good Indian was a dead one, shot on sight, while the Indians in turn raided white settlements, scalping and torturing wherever they went. Treaties were made and broken, with the Indians generally getting the worst of it. It was the age-old story of a vigorous new race annihilating or driving out the weaker side. The white settlers wanted the land, and the Indians had to go. Naturally they resented it, and thus began the series of Indian wars and massacres which stained with human blood almost every page of mountain history.

Here is the official report of the Battle of Island Flats. It gives us a realistic picture of the ferocity and lust for blood which always accompanied these Indian fights:

On the 19th our scouts returned and informed us that they had discovered where a great number of Indians were making into the settlements, upon which alarm the few men stationed at Eaton's completed a breastwork sufficiently strong, with the assistance of what men were there, to have repelled a considerable number; sent expresses to the different stations and collected all the forces in one body, and the morning after about one hundred and seventy turned out in search of the enemy. We marched in two divisions with flankers on either side and scouts before. Our scouts discovered upwards of twenty meeting us, and fired on them. They returned the fire, but our men rushed on with such violence that they were obliged to make a precipitate retreat. We took ten bundles and a good deal of plunder, and had great reason to think that some of them were wounded. This small skirmish happened on ground very disadvantageous for our men to pursue, though it was with the greatest difficulty our officers could restrain their men. A council was held and it was thought advisable to return, as we imagined there was a large party not far off. We accordingly returned and had not marched more than a mile when a number, not inferior to ours, attacked us in the rear. Our men sustained the attack with great bravery and intrepidity, immediately forming a line. The Indians endeavored to surrounded us, but were prevented by the uncommon fortitude and vigilance of Captain James Shelby, who took possession of an eminence that prevented their design. Our line of battle extended about a quarter of a mile. We killed about thirteen on the spot, whom we found, and we have the greatest reason to believe that we could have found a great many more had we had time to search for them. There were streams of blood everywhere, and it was generally thought there was never so much execution done in so short a time on the frontiers. Never did troops fight with greater calmness than ours did. The Indians attacked us with the greatest fury imaginable and made the most vigorous efforts to

surround us.   Our spies really deserve the greatest
applause.   We took a great deal of plunder and
many guns, and had only four men greatly wounded.
The rest of the troops are in high spirits and eager
for another engagement.   We have the greatest
reason to believe they are pouring in in great num-
bers on us, and beg the assistance of our friends.

| | |
|---|---|
| JAMES THOMPSON | JOHN CAMPBELL |
| JAMES SHELBY | WILLIAM COOKE |
| WILLIAM BUCHANAN | THOMAS MADISON |

The mountains were dotted over with
little forts, into which the settlers gathered
whenever an attack was expected.   The
following description of one of the frontier
forts is taken from *Tennessee History Stories:*

A fort was made by setting heavy timbers upright
in the ground so as to enclose an acre or more with
a wooden wall.   Sometimes a row of cabins formed
a part of the wall.   At one or more corners of the
fort was a blockhouse.

A blockhouse was built up higher than the walls
of the fort and reached beyond the top of the walls.
This was to allow those inside to shoot down through
the floor and along the sides of the walls in case
anyone tried to climb over the defences or set fire
to the fort.

Inside the walls of the fort, cabins were built for
living rooms, bedrooms, kitchens, and storehouses.

Each redskin who wriggled through the small hole fell without a sound

A large fort had so much in it that it would remind you of a small village.

In the blockhouses there were holes in the walls through which the riflemen fired upon the Indians when they made their attacks. In time of war you would scarcely dare to look out through one of these portholes. If you did, you might be killed by an Indian bullet.

There was a big door, or gate, at one side of the fort. Through this everything was brought into the enclosure. In times of danger and always at night, the gate was closed. A large beam passed across it and rested in strong sockets, to make the gate secure. Sometimes it was made fast with a big chain.

When no Indians were near, the gates were opened in the morning and the settlers went out to work. Their fields were near by, but someone always stood guard while the others plowed or reaped. Indian corn was the principal crop.

The Indians often attacked these forts. The usual method was first to cut off the water supply, which very often was isolated from the fort, and then with burning arrows to set fire to the building. In most instances the besieged frontiersmen were able to hold out until help came. Failing this, they generally fought to the last man, preferring death to the certainty of dreadful torture.

Often the Indians stalked in the woods and picked off the workers in the field. More often they attacked isolated cabins, hoping to take the occupants unaware before they had time to reach the shelter of the fort. As the men were often away, it sometimes fell to the women to defend the homes. There were loopholes in almost every cabin, and those wonderful pioneer women knew how to load and fire the muzzle-loader.

There are many true stories of how they defended their homes and their children successfully against savage Indian attacks. In 1791, in Nelson County, Kentucky, a number of Indians attacked the Merrill cabin, which was isolated in the forest, far away from the nearest fort. The attack was swiftly delivered and relentlessly pressed home. The family were completely surprised. A shot rang out, followed by some savage Indian yells, and the father, who was pulling out stumps near the house, fell, seriously wounded. With a desperate effort, he got up and half crawled, half staggered, to the cabin, where his wife, who kept her head, caught him as he collapsed, dragged him inside, and slammed and barred the heavy door right in the face of the foremost Indian.

Their lives and those of their two children now depended upon her. It looked hopeless, with only one woman against over twenty armed savages. She had no gun— her husband was too badly wounded to reach for it when he fell. The only weapon of defense in the cabin was an ax. She seized it and grimly waited until the Indians commenced to chop down the door. She stood silently to one side with the ax uplifted. As redskin after redskin wriggled through the small hole, she crashed the ax down on his skull, and he fell without a sound. The rear Indians, suspicious that something was wrong, abandoned the frontal attack, clambered up on the roof and proceeded to wriggle down the chimney. The brave pioneer mother, realizing what they were up to, ordered the two children to throw the big feather mattress on the fire while she remained on guard at the door. Clouds of thick, pungent smoke and tongues of flame leaped up the chimney and brought down the two Indians, half suffocated, badly scorched and stunned. As they rolled out on the hearthstone, the mother dispatched them too. Another attempted to wriggle through the hole in the door; and for the seventh time the ax connected.

That was too much, even for Indians. They hastily withdrew, and upon their return to the wigwam complained that the squaws were harder fighters and infinitely more ferocious than the "Long Knives" themselves.

The Indians always referred to the frontiersmen as "Long Knives." The name in all probability came from the fact that the first soldiers to invade the wilderness were armed with swords in contrast to the stone weapons which the Indians originally carried.

Often young boys distinguished themselves in fights with the Indians. Hardy Goodfellow in his early youth lived and hunted with Daniel Boone. Long before he was twenty years of age, he had many scalps dangling from his belt.

An early pioneer built his log cabin on the banks of the Ohio River, across which the forest was full of redskins who lurked in ambush, hoping to pick off any lone hunter or trapper. The pioneer, who knew their ways and never underestimated their skill, warned his son, a boy of fourteen, on no account ever to go across to the opposite bank.

One morning the youngster told his father that he had heard some wild turkeys "gobbling" over there and asked permission to cross over and have a shot at them. The father, knowing only too well that the Indians often imitated turkeys and other birds and animals in order to attract hunters, forbade the boy to go and sternly ordered him to remain at home.

That afternoon while the father was out working on the farm, the son quietly and quickly canoed across the river and plunged into the forest after the turkeys. While stealthily proceeding through the trees, with his eyes carefully observing everything and with every nerve on the alert, he suddenly saw the feathered head of an Indian appear above a log one hundred yards away. The father had been right after all. The boy's blood froze in his veins. He was panic-stricken and wanted to run, but only for a

moment.   He was the true son of a pioneer.
Realizing that the Indian was still too far
away to shoot at him, he acted as if he had
not noticed anything unusual and calmly
proceeded to hunt for the turkey.   At the
same time he watched the "brave" out of
the corner of his eye and slowly and quietly
circled away through the trees until he was
behind him, when he carefully sighted and
fired.   The redskin leaped high in the air,
and with the war whoop of his tribe gurgling
in his throat, pitched forward dead, with
the boy's bullet through his body.

Returning home, the boy related the
incident to his father, who merely smiled
and dismissed it as the fantastic imagining
of a young boy.   But when the youngster
the next day still insisted, the father quietly
crossed over and found the Indian exactly
where the son said that he had killed him.

Invariably the redskins scalped their
victims.   They simply gripped the hair in
their fingers and with a sharp cutting knife
skinned off the top of the head.   There are
several instances of settlers being scalped
and living and returning to their friends.
The story is told that young David Hood

went out, with two other boys, to a place
a few miles from the fort at French Lick.
On their return journey that evening they
ran into Indians, who wounded them.
Young Hood rolled and hid in the canebrake. When the redskins found him, he
shammed dead. He figured that they would
not bother him. He was right up to a certain
point. But one of the Indians thought he
might as well have the boy's scalp, and
seizing him by the hair commenced hacking
away at the top of his head. What the
boy's feelings were it is not hard to imagine.
But, knowing that his life depended upon
it, he endured the agony without making
a single movement or emitting one groan.
The Indians then left him.

Half unconscious and covered with blood,
he rose, peered through the cane, and, seeing
no Indians, walked, or rather reeled toward
the fort. He was so weak from loss of
blood and the excruciating pain of the
scalping that he mistook his directions and
again blundered into the Indians, who
laughingly yelled to him that a dead man
could not walk. Just to make sure, they
put a bullet through his breast; and to

complete the ghastly business, plunged their knives into him on all sides and threw his body into a brush pile. There was a freeze that night, and to add to his agony, cold gripped and froze him to the marrow of his bones. The following day his friends came out of the fort, and trailing him by his own blood, found his half frozen, unconscious body. Thinking him dead, they prepared for the funeral. While they were dressing the body, he began to moan. "Aren't you dead?" inquired some of his friends. Hood sat up and weakly answered, "No, I am not, if you will only give me a chance."

The favorite form of Indian torture was the "slow fire." The wretched victim was tied to a stake with dry brushwood piled in a wide circle around his feet. After the children and the squaws tired themselves out spitting in his face and jeering and laughing at him, the warriors began to apply such artistic touches as whizzing tomahawks past his head, shooting arrows into his limbs, and other diabolical forms of Indian amusement. After they were tired out, the fire was started. While the braves

Daniel Boone was the trail blazer, the "voice crying in the wilderness"

in their war paints danced what was called
the stake dance, the victim was slowly
roasted to death.

Blood calls for blood. That was the code
of the frontier. The white man immediately sent out punitive expeditions, which
shot down the Indians on sight, burned
their villages, and devastated their corn
patches.

Daniel Boone was one of the few frontiersmen who understood the redskins and who
was very highly regarded by them. He
could out-Indian any Indian who ever
roamed the forest. On one occasion he was
standing on the bluffs above the Ohio River,
hundreds of miles away from the nearest
white settlement. The sun was setting and
touching the forest with gold as far as the
eye could see. Boone was not only a fearless hunter and a great fighter, but was also
inspired with the vision of the statesman.
He was the trail blazer, the "voice crying in
the wilderness." He always showed the
way and then moved on to the new and the
unknown. On this particular occasion he
was probably visualizing the future state of
Kentucky. Or maybe with the eyes of a

poet—and he was a poet—was marveling over the sunset in the virgin forest. Anyway, while he was standing there dreaming, some Indians crept stealthily through the trees and rushed him. Their hands were almost on him, when suddenly he dived headfirst over the bluff, landed in some trees below, clutched desperately at their branches, eased his fall, and squirrel-like, wriggled, swung away, and disappeared.

More than any other man who ever lived, he knew the Indians' ways and understood their primitive psychology. He could follow their trails and catch up with them no matter what pains they took to cover their tracks.

On one occasion his daughter, Jemima, with her two friends, Betsey and Fannie Calloway, were canoeing on the Kentucky River, when a swift current seized their canoe and swept it down the river and against the opposite bank, where five Shawnee braves who were hiding in ambush in the bushes waded out and captured them. The screams of the girls attracted the notice of Boone and the others at the fort. A posse headed by the fathers was organized

immediately and set out in pursuit. The
Indians, knowing they would be pursued,
cunningly tried to leave no trail and em-
ployed every device they knew to elude
their pursuers. The girls—and they were
the worthy daughters of pioneers—tore
their clothing and left little pieces every few
hundred yards. This was enough for Boone.
For two days he relentlessly followed and
at the end of that time came upon the
abductors. He knew, though, if he attempted to rush them they would in all
probability kill the girls and escape through
the forest. Controlling his urge to leap at
them and exact vengeance, he persuaded
his companions to hide near by while he
quietly and carefully reconnoitered. After
sundown, when the Indians were sleeping,
with the captured and tied girls near by,
he and his companions rushed the camp,
killed two of the Shawnees, drove the others
off, and rescued the girls.

On another occasion, in 1777, while he
and his companions were out in the wilderness gathering salt, he was ambushed and
surprised by four burly Shawnees. He
tried to outrun them—in vain. Their

bullets whanged past his ears.  He surrendered.  They tied and conducted him
to camp, where he was received by over
one hundred warriors under Chief Black
Fish.  The Indians had a very high regard
for Daniel Boone and refrained from torturing or in any way molesting him.
Nevertheless, they watched him closely,
and despite his pleas, refused to unbind and
allow him to return to his comrades.  From
their conversation, he quickly learned that
they were planning an immediate attack on
the fort at Boonesborough.  This was
the white man's farthest outpost in Kentucky, and inasmuch as most of the frontiersmen were away gathering salt, the
guardians of the fort would be able to offer
little resistance to the band of warring
Indians.

Lying by the camp fire in the center of
the braves, with his hands and feet securely
tied, and with no possible chance of escape,
he reviewed the situation mentally.  He
knew the shiftless nature of the Indians,
and figured that they would be satisfied
with a few "palefaces."  Accordingly, he
agreed to lead them to the camp at the salt

licks and guaranteed that in return for good treatment, his fellow salt makers would surrender and go north with their captors, where they would be ransomed for twenty dollars a head by the British authorities in Detroit. He also assured them that he would be perfectly willing to be adopted by the tribe and spend the remainder of his life living and hunting in their midst. The Indians agreed. The plan worked. The salt makers were captured and later on turned over for the ransom money to Governor Hamilton. But they refused to release Boone even when the Governor offered one hundred pounds for him, and escorted him back to their hunting grounds, where he lived as one of them. Months later, while out with the braves hunting wild turkey, he escaped, and after a perilous journey arrived at the fort at Boonesborough.

Unquestionably his marvelous understanding of the ways of the redskins saved his own life and ultimately that of his companions and protected the almost defenseless fort from a surprise attack and a massacre.

Big Sam Houston, who years later in the greatest comeback in American history, was to save Texas, was under Old Hickory in his worst Indian fights.   In a mix-up with the redskins an arrow pierced his thigh. He tried to pull it out, but it would not come.   He halted a lieutenant who was passing and asked him to pull it out for him.   The officer pulled hard enough, but the barbed arrow stuck fast.   Whereupon, the officer told Houston to report to a surgeon.   Maddened with pain and determined at all costs to get the arrow out, he drew his sword and commanded the lieutenant to try again.   The officer did so and succeeded, but the arrow left a terrible gash. Suffering dreadfully from pain, weakened by loss of blood and vomiting, he staggered away and had the horrible wound plugged up.   Andrew Jackson visited him and ordered him not to return to the battle. That afternoon, when the fight was raging with an intensity of fury, he returned to his command and led the attack against the Indian stronghold.   A bullet shattered his right arm and another broke his right shoulder.   Despite this, he continued to

rally and lead his men until from sheer loss
of blood he fainted.

Sam Houston, according to Judge Jo C.
Guild, "stood six feet in his socks, was of
fine contour, a remarkably well propor-
tioned man, and of commanding and gallant
bearing; had a large, long head and face,
and his fine features were lit up by large
eagle-looking eyes; possessed of a wonderful
recollection of persons and names, a fine
address and courtly manners and a magnet-
ism approaching that of General Andrew
Jackson. He enjoyed unbounded popular-
ity among men and was a great favorite
with the ladies."

He knew and understood the redskins.
He had spent much of his boyhood in their
wigwams; and when, with a broken heart,
he resigned his office and walked out of the
governor's mansion in Nashville, he turned
his back upon all white men and threw in
his lot with the Cherokees. He lived with
them for years, slept in their wigwams,
wore their clothes, joined in their hunts,
and married an Indian wife. Oo-loo-te-ka,
the famous chief of the Cherokees, welcomed
him with these words: "My son, eleven

winters have passed since we met. I have heard you were a great chief among your people. I have heard that a dark cloud has fallen on the white path you would walk. I am glad of it—it is done by the Great Spirit. We are in trouble, and the Great Spirit has sent you to us to give us counsel. My wigwam is yours—my home is yours—rest with us."

Sam Houston often said in later years that when he laid himself down to sleep that night he felt like a weary wanderer returned at last to his father's house. He loved and understood the Indians. Again and again he went to Washington to petition the Government in their behalf.

Here is an extract from a letter to his friend, President Andrew Jackson: "To ameliorate the conditions of the Indians, to prevent fraud and peculations on the part of the Government agents among them, and to direct the feelings of the Indians in kindness to the Government and inspire them with confidence in its justice and magnanimity toward the red people, have been the bases of my constant solicitude and attention since I have been among them."

A typical log cabin with roughhewn logs, puncheon floor, and clapboard roof

He left them at last to go to Texas to avenge Davy Crockett and the other heroes who had died at the Alamo, to overthrow and capture Santa Anna, the Mexican dictator, and to win the Lone Star State for the Union. But he never forgot the kindness of the Indians and always remained their loyal friend and stalwart champion.

Here is the most eloquent Indian speech on record. John Logan, who delivered it, was the famous chief of the Shawnees. His family had been wantonly murdered by border ruffians, as a result of which he dug up the tomahawk, sent the war pipe through all of the neighboring villages, and began a wholesale massacre of the pale-faces. This led to what is known in American history as Dunmore's War:

I appeal to any white man to say if ever he entered Logan's cabin hungry and he gave him not meat; if ever he came cold and naked and he clothed him not. During the course of the last long and bloody war, Logan remained idle in his camp, an advocate of peace. Such was my love for the whites that my countrymen pointed as I passed and said: "Logan is the friend of the white man." I had even thought to have lived with you, but for the injuries of one

man.   Colonel Cresap, the last spring, in cold blood
and unprovoked, murdered all the relations of
Logan, not even sparing my women and children.
There runs not a drop of my blood in the veins of
any living creature.   This called on me for revenge.
I have sought it.   I have killed many.   I have
fully glutted my vengeance.   For my country I
rejoice at the beams of peace; but do not harbor
a thought that mine is a joy of fear.   Logan never
felt it.   He will not turn on his heel to save his
life.   Who is there to mourn for Logan?   Not one.

There can be no question about it that
the white man, too, shared the responsibility for these Indian fights.   Honest traders
were few and far between.   As we have
said before, too often treaties were broken,
promises not lived up to, and bad bargains
struck.   Often the Indians surrendered a
buffalo robe, some valuable pelt, or a
valuable beaver or otter skin for a paltry
string of beads or a small tube of worthless
red paint.

Theodore Roosevelt, in his *Winning of
the West*, gives both sides:

The history of the border wars, both in the ways
they began and in the ways they were waged, makes
a long tale of injuries inflicted, suffered, and merci-
lessly revenged.

It could not be otherwise when brutal, reckless
and lawless borderers, despising all men not their
own color, were thrown in contact with savages who
esteemed cruelty and treachery as the highest
virtues, and rapine and murder as the worthiest of
pursuits.

Moreover, it was sadly inevitable that the law-
abiding borderer, as well as the white ruffian, the
peaceful Indian as well as the painted marauder,
should be plunged into the struggle to suffer the
punishment that should only have fallen on their
evil-minded fellows.

Looking back, it is easy to say that much of the
wrongdoing could have been prevented, but if we
examine the facts to find out the truth, not to estab-
lish a theory, we are bound to admit that the struggle
was really one that could not possibly have been
avoided.

Mere outrages could be atoned for or settled, the
question which lay at the root of our difficulties was
that of the occupation of the land itself, and to
this there could be no solution save war.   The
Indians had no ownership of land in the way in
which we understand the term.   The tribes lived
far apart; each had for its hunting grounds all the
territory from which it was not barred by rivals.
Each looked with jealousy upon all interlopers when
occasion offered.   Every good hunting ground was
claimed by many nations.   It was rare, indeed, that
any tribe had an uncontested title to a large tract
of land;  where such title existed it rested not on

actual occupancy and cultivation, but on the recent butchery of the weaker rivals.   For instance, there were a dozen tribes, all of whom hunted in Kentucky, and fought each other there, all of whom had equally good titles to the soil, and not one of whom acknowledged the right of any other.   As a matter of fact, they had therein no right, save the right of the strongest.   The land no more belonged to them than it belonged to Boone and the white hunters who first visited it.*

---

*From *The Winning of the West*, by Theodore Roosevelt. Copyright by G. P. Putnam's Sons.   Quoted by courtesy of the publishers.

## Chapter V

## Log Cabins

THE log cabins of the pioneers were the outposts of civilization. They tell more plainly than the historian the heroic story of the conquering of the wilderness. They are distinctly, uniquely American. Many of the greatest Americans that ever lived were born within their roughhewn walls. Abraham Lincoln, Andrew Jackson, Daniel Boone, David Crockett, and Sam Houston first saw the light of day in log cabins.

The intrepid pioneers broke trails through the wilderness, and far away from civilization searched for a site for their new homes. They sought a place with plenty of game, good soil, running water, and timber. These were indispensable. Upon finding such a location, the first thing the pioneer did was to build his log cabin. Even isolated in the wilderness, he had to have his home.

(67)

Because of prowling Indians and chance marauders, the home had to be stoutly built and almost a fort. The cabins were constructed of round logs. Sometimes they were "scalped"; that is, roughly hewn, or dressed with ordinary axes. Sometimes the hard earth, well beaten down, served for a floor. Sometimes split logs were used. These were called puncheon floors. The roof was constructed of clapboards, held in place by small logs. Generally there was only one room, with one door and one window. Heavy shutters guarded these two openings. In many of the cabins there were loopholes where rifles could be thrust through in the event of an attack.

The furniture, of course, was handmade and primitive. Beds were made by sticking two poles in the chinks of the wall, with the opposite ends resting in rough forks cut from the branches of the trees. Flat boards were placed across them to support the bed tick, which was stuffed with leaves or straw. The fireplace and chimney were very important. There was plenty of wood for fuel, and in the winter time roaring fires blazed in almost every cabin. Fireplaces were built of rough stones or slabs chinked with clay. Chimneys were constructed of wooden slabs lined with mortar or mud. The most popular lamp was a wick floating in a bowl of bear grease.

The pioneers preferred to build their cabins close to a fresh-water spring; and as the springs were often miles apart, the settlements generally were widely dispersed through the forest.

The pioneers had to make their own clothes. Sometimes the womenfolk brought a spinning wheel with them, and on a long winter's night carded and wove and spun the rough homespun so popular in the forest. More often they made their clothes from the skins of the animals. A doeskin properly dressed made an excellent hunting shirt and, when bordered with panther hair or the fur of the bear, looked picturesque as well as serviceable. The belt which held it close to the body was made of dyed and tanned buffalo hide, with sheathes for the hunting knife and the tomahawk. Coon and fox skins were popular for making caps.   The tail of the animal was always left on the cap and hung jauntily down the back.   Moccasins for the feet were made of soft buffalo hide.   They were waterproof, adapted themselves to the shape of the feet, and at the same time permitted the wearer to slip noiselessly through the forest.   Buffalo robes were used for overcoats.

## CHAPTER VI

## Muzzle-Loaders

LIVING in the wilderness, subject at any moment to Indian attacks, and having to hunt and kill his food, the pioneer had to be an expert shot, have a rifle he could depend upon, and an ever-ready supply of ammunition. The long muzzle-loader, with the powderhorn and soft doeskin pouch full of balls, was a familiar sight in every log cabin.

Like the log cabins, these muzzle-loaders are distinctly American.

When men like Boone, Crockett, and the Long Hunters penetrated the wilderness, their lives depended upon their rifles. They had to have guns which used a minimum of ammunition, made very little noise, and could be reloaded quickly and shot with reasonable accuracy. A flash-back, a jammed barrel, or faulty percussion would be fatal in a fight with an Indian. His tomahawk would be buried in the hunter's brain long before he had a chance to "doctor the sick rifle." It was very dangerous, too, to face a wounded bear or buffalo without a firearm which was absolutely dependable.

There were no such rifles in the world. The old European flintlocks, muskets, and blunderbusses were all right for the continental wars. A miss did not matter so much over there; accuracy of aim was not entirely necessary; and there was plenty of ammunition. This sort of thing, however, would never do in the American wilderness.

Unable to secure the sort of rifles they must have, the pioneers made their own. Throughout the mountains you can still see the ruins of the old blast furnaces they used. They dug the soft ore from the mountains, forged it into steel, and either welded or bored out the barrels and then rifled them or grooved them spirally. Trigger, trigger guard, firing pan, flintlock, sights, and all the other fittings were also made on the spot. The stock was generally carved from grained and seasoned wood, such as bird's-eye maple, curly cherry, or black walnut.

The best known rifles were the Gibsons, the Beans, and the Duncans. The Decherds, too, were very popular.

Daniel Boone's rifle, which is still in existence, weighed eleven pounds, was five feet four inches long, and fired a round ball that weighed fifty-five to the pound—a little heavier than a 32 Winchester. He was so expert that he could reload walking, running, or at a gallop on horseback, in less than ten seconds.

Davy Crockett's rifle, "Betsey," was a long, smooth-bored muzzle-loader of the best Pennsylvania workmanship.

To us who live in the twentieth century and are accustomed to modern high-powered rifles, these long, heavy, old-fashioned muzzle-loaders appear stupid and clumsy, and we naturally wonder why, when the pioneers had to carry them on their long hunts, they should have been so big and heavy. As a matter of fact, they were perfectly adapted for the conditions under which the pioneer lived. They used very little powder—about half the weight of the ball. The reason for the length and thickness of the barrel was accuracy of aim.

The first shot had to hit the mark, or it was unfortunate for the hunter or fighter. The Indian was generally on top of him before he could reload, or the game had bounded off through the forest.

The thick barrel tremendously increased the accuracy of the shooting by eliminating the "whip"; that is, the variation. A small charge of powder and the length and thickness of the barrel combined reduced the recoil to a minimum. When the gun was fired from the shoulder, this did not matter very much, but when fired from the thigh, or from under the arm, when the shooter was hiding behind a tree or running through the forest, this reduction of the recoil was very important.

The mountaineers could not only make their own guns, but they generally carried spare parts, and could effectively repair them if anything went wrong. They preferred French powder to any other, but in case of necessity they could manufacture their own. On almost every mountain side there is a saltpeter cave where they made it.

The pioneers took great care of their rifles. They had to. Their lives depended on it. They guarded the firing pan against dampness and rain with a sleeve which was slipped down over the barrel. It was usually a round piece of hide skinned from the leg of an elk or a buffalo. Out in the wilderness they usually slept with their rifles between their legs so that nobody could take them away from them. If they were forced to climb trees to orient themselves, they generally hid their rifles under logs, or in the brush where the Indians could not find them.

After a little practice the loading of these rifles became a simple matter. The gun was placed upright with the butt resting on the ground. The powder was poured from the powderhorn, which was made from the horn of a buck or a steer, into the charger or measurer, which was the tip of an elk's horn. The amount of powder used depended to a great extent upon the distance of the shot. A long shot naturally required a bigger charge of powder than a short one. The powder was then poured down the muzzle of the gun. Next, a small patch, which usually was cut from an old piece of cloth and smeared with bear grease, was placed over the end of the muzzle, after which the ball was taken out of the shot pouch and pressed with the thumb into the barrel.  The ends of the patch were trimmed off and the ball driven down the barrel with a ramrod, which was generally a piece of hickory which had been whittled into shape.  A couple of jabs with the ramrod packed the ball into place.  The patch lay on top of the powder and packed the ball tight so that the explosion could not possibly escape.  After that it was a case of good eyesight, steady nerves, and experience.

## CHAPTER VII

# Mountaineers

THE modern mountaineers are direct descendants of pioneers who settled the mountains over a hundred years ago, whipping the Indians, taming the wilderness, killing off the big game, and stringing their log cabins across Appalachia from the Great Smokies to the Cumberlands.

Theirs is wild, picturesque country, with towering mountains, bare hills, water in abundance, long, low valleys, coves where razorbacks grub for acorns, and ravines where scrub cattle with jangling bells hanging on their necks forage out a meager existence. There are rocks and trees everywhere, timber ripe for the ax, sawmills whining and clanging, and great yawning caves where bushwhackers and feudists often manufactured gunpowder and whiskey.

It is beautiful country, with mountain laurel, white patches of dogwood blossoms, redbud, gorgeous rhododendrons, and wild flowers of every color and variety.

They have never had very much money. There used to be no good roads in or out—only creek beds and mountain trains.  Once they got into the mountains, they usually stayed.  The outside world moved on from the eighteenth to the nineteenth to the twentieth century, while the mountaineers continued to live the primitive eighteenth-century life of their Scotch-Irish ancestors. They are over a hundred years behind the times.

With few exceptions they are red-headed, rawboned, and gangling—the true Anglo-Saxon type.  The men wear jeans or over-alls, and quite a number of the women wear linsey dresses and split bonnets. There are very, very few colored people in the mountains, and practically no foreigners.

Like their forefathers, they are very resourceful.  I know many mountaineers who can make rifles and doctor sick ones, and who are blacksmiths, cobblers, car-penters, farmers, traders, and a number of other things.  I know many mountain women who can card, weave, spin, make soap, cook, do dressmaking, and even plow and harrow.

To this day they are God-fearing men and women. Their God is still the God of the Old Testament. They have just as much abhorrence as their ancestors had for rituals, liturgies, rosaries, and prayer books. Fire-and-brimstone evangelists threatening sinners with all the terrors of hell's flames and promising the faithful angels' wings and pearly gates are very popular in the mountains. They are always certain of big crowds, enthusiastic receptions, and a rich crop of "redeemed souls." The saddle-bagger, with his saddlebags stuffed with Bibles, still rides the circuit, away back in the mountains.

The mountaineers love liberty with a fanatical zeal. They will tolerate no political bosses. It is impossible to tell which way they are going to vote. That is why the mountain states are referred to as the doubtful states. After the last Presidental election I asked a mountaineer if he had voted for Hoover.

He answered in the negative.

"Smith then?"

He shook his head.

"Then whom did you vote for?" I insisted.

He looked at me for a while, and in that quiet, smooth voice of the typical mountaineer, answered: "No! I didn't vote for them thar men, simply because I was ordered to. But to show my political independence I went to the polls and voted for Old Hickory again."

The mountaineers take their politics seriously, but they very much resent being told for whom they should or should not vote.

Modern jazz has not penetrated the mountains to any great extent, and the mountain folk still sing the beautiful old border ballads which their ancestors brought over. The English singers on their recent tour of this country presented a group of Appalachian folk songs which blended in beautifully with their old English songs.

No mountaineer ever says "it." He says "hit," just as Chaucer and Shakespeare did. He very often says "ye" instead of "you." He says "we-uns" and "you-uns," even as Chaucer did in his *Canterbury Tales* and Shakespeare in *A Winter's Tale*. He uses nouns as adjectives and adjectives as nouns, which is very, very old Anglo-Saxon. He says "rifle-gun," "hound-dog," "ham-meat," "corn-bread," "neighbor-folk," "cow-brute" and "preacher-man." He very often makes a plural by adding an unnecessary *es*. For instance, the mountaineer says "women" and "womenses"; "guns" and "gunses"; and "dogs" and "dogses."

He uses the affirmative and the negative with telling effect. I once asked a mountaineer to do something for me, something important. A couple of days later when I met him I asked if it had been done. He looked at me, and quietly but emphatically answered, "Hit's done done."

Then I knew it was done.

Here are some mountain negatives—"ain't," "ain't never," "ain't never done," "ain't never done nothin'," "ain't never done nothin' nohow." A fight is always referred to as a "fray," which is also Old English. "I am afraid" is "I'm afeared." If the weather is going to clear up, "Hit's a-goin' to fair up." A long way is referred to as "a right fur piece." The new moon is always "the soon o' the moon." Some time ago while out hunting with a mountaineer we stirred up a fox, which he wanted me to head off. Instead of saying "Hurry up," he used the mountain expression, "You'd better get a soon go." When two mountaineers meet, they generally greet each other with the inevitable "Howdy?" The answer generally is "Tol'able."

## Chapter VIII

# Feudists

THE mountaineers are clansmen. Family ties count for everything. An insult to one member is regarded as an insult to the whole. Every member regards it as his solemn duty to avenge it.

The absence of good highways, railroads, and well-organized telephone service makes the administration of justice slow and difficult. For a long time, mountaineers have preferred to settle their disputes in their own way.

The mountains being isolated and far from the "madding crowd," it is only natural that lawless people, afraid of capture and punishment in the more settled sections, have retreated to their fastnesses and made their homes there. Some of them, renouncing their old ways, have turned out to be decent, law-abiding citizens. Others have attempted to continue their lawlessness. It is indeed difficult for the Ethiopian to change his skin or the leopard its spots.

These three reasons, together with the natural pugnacity and fearless individualism of the mountaineer explain, although they do not vindicate, the bloody feuds. These feuds have splotched the mountains with human blood, taken hundreds of lives, ruined much property, and shocked the more law-abiding people of the nation.

In spite of what has been done to color these feuds with romance and chivalry, the fact remains that they have always been cruel, senseless, savage, and very often cowardly murders. It is difficult to see any chivalry in a dead shot's crouching in ambush in a canebrake and cold-bloodedly shooting his enemy in the back as he passes. It is even more difficult to extract romance from a night raid where a half dozen armed men suddenly descend upon an isolated cabin in the mountains and savagely and deliberately murder unarmed people. This has occurred not once, but many, many times in these feuds. Occasionally feudists met face to face, took the law into their own hands, and shot each other down.

More often a sudden shot in the back, a treacherous knife thrust, or a sudden attack in which the odds were in favor of the attackers, was the usual method of the killers.

Outsiders, provided they minded their own business, were seldom molested. Only blood relations and sympathizers were marked and tracked down and killed.

Hatred, revenge, lawlessness, murder, ambush, and assassination—all these cruel, barbarous, and primitive emotions and actions were associated with the feuds.

Often the whole business has started over some trivial incident. The fierce Hatfield-McCoy feud in Pike County, Kentucky, had its origin in an argument over some hogs. One of the Hatfields had been fattening some razorbacks in the acorn groves in the mountains. He drove them into Springtown, Kentucky, and put them in a pen there. A few days later one of the McCoys saw them, swore they were his, and demanded that they be turned over to him instantly. First, there were arguments and lawsuits. Then there was bloodshed. Somebody lost his head in an argument or refused to accept the legal decision and "shot up" one of the opposing side. Blood calls for blood. The members of the dead man's family retaliated by ambushing and trying to kill the killer. Failing to find him, they shot down other members of his family who happened along. Passions rose. There were more killings, until every blood relation on both sides was drawn into the feud and marked for a merciless death. The peace of the mountains was disturbed for several years. Many of the killers were arrested and tried, but only one was ever hanged.

Moonshine and politics started the Tolliver-Martin-Logan feud in Roane County, Tennessee. Wild cats could not have been more treacherous toward each other than they were and could not have fought more savagely. For years they knifed and shot each other until it is a wonder that any of them were left. The officers of the law were either afraid to go into the mountains after them, or else were corrupted. Juries were bribed; justice was suspended. All this happened just because a number of hotheads considered themselves above the law

David Crockett

General Sam Houston

and decided on account of some trivial insult to burn and murder every member of the opposite side.

Claims have been made that the feudists sincerely believed that they were solemnly obligated to take the law into their own hands in this way. So much the worse for them. "Vengeance is mine," saith the Lord. Very often they paid with their lives or property for their primitive and mistaken ideas of honor.

It would take an entire book, or many books, to write the history of these disgraceful and bloodthirsty mountain feuds.

Fortunately, good roads, schools, and the influence of the more decent mountaineers have minimized these feuds. Today wholesale killings are few and far between.

## Chapter IX

## Mother York

THE blacksmith who died from the effects of the mule kick was a typical mountaineer. He was a splendid shot and a great hunter. He lived in the midst of the moonshiners but never drank. Nor was he ever involved in the feuds. Boone and Crockett, Houston and Old Hickory were living realities with him. He had heard so much about them that he felt that he really knew them. He talked of them as though they still lived. All the folklore of the mountains was stored up in his mind, and on long winter nights, before the open fireplace, or out in the woods on the trail of foxes or deer, he retold it to his children. This was their patrimony.

His wife was equally picturesque, and after his death continued to nurture her fledglings in the heroic tales of the past. Mother York, as she is affectionately called in the mountains, is truly a wonderful

woman. The last time I was down there I
spent much of my time visiting and talking
with her. She usually sat in front of the
fireplace, in a linsey dress and split bonnet,
and looked very much like those wonderful
women who went West in covered wagons
long ago.

"What is your philosophy of life?" I
asked her one day.

She looked at me with a face as wise and
wrinkled as old parchment. Her eyes
beamed, and she half smiled as she replied:
"I hain't had much o' the larnin' that
comes out o' books, but I brung up by the
hair of the head, all alone, in a one-room
log cabin, eleven red-headed kids; and
they're all alive and well today; and thet
larns you somethin' about livin'."

Napoleon once said that everything he
ever achieved he owed to his mother. Alvin York with truth could say the same
thing.

Mother York was born during the Civil
War, when hatreds were at their highest
pitch, blood was shed on the slightest
provocation, and men killed and houses
burned all over the mountains. Guerillas

and bushwhackers roamed and ravaged everywhere. The border states suffered frightfully. The tides of battle ebbed and flowed over them for years, breaking in bloody surf against once peaceful towns and quiet homes.

Mother York's father was killed by the bushwhackers in Jamestown when she was only a little baby in her mother's arms. They hooked him to the tail of a mule, dragged him through the streets, and riddled him with bullets. Shortly after this terrible atrocity, a little baby brother came into the world. The mother never married again. In her simple mountain cabin she reared her babies and lovingly and intelligently guided them to manhood and womanhood. She was Sergeant York's grandmother.

His mother, to whom we refer in this book as "Mother York," is certainly the heroic type, a true pioneer, a born leader, and a wise and loving counselor—the sort of woman who, under more advantageous circumstances, by the sheer force of her courage and personality, would have made her mark in the world.

When I asked her how she was able to
bring up eleven children, all alone in a one-
room log cabin fifty miles from the nearest
railroad, she smiled and naïvely informed
me that she "just turned them loose on
the mountain side like a litter of young
razorbacks."

When I asked her why Alvin was the
biggest of them all, she looked lovingly at
him, laughed, and answered, "When he
was young, I whipped him that much that
I kept his skin loose and he had plenty of
room to fill out." That was too much for
the outstanding hero of the World War.
He looked at her, and, fearful of what she
was going to say next, slipped out through
the door, grinned, and disappeared.

When her illustrious son returned from
France, the citizens of Nashville gave him
a tremendous public reception. Everybody
who was anybody was there. Mother York
was invited. She positively refused to
wear city clothes, or any other such "con-
traptions," as she called them, and appeared
among them neatly garbed in a simple
linsey dress, fringed shawl, and split bonnet.
A pioneer woman, an eighteenth century

character in the midst of that glittering assembly, the simplicity of her character and the innate modesty and dignity of her personality instantly won their hearts. So tremendous was the appeal she made to all present that a guard had to be formed about her to relieve the pressure of the enthusiastic, hand-shaking people who thronged and milled around, anxious to pay tribute to this glorified mother who brought with her the wholesomeness of the backwoods and all the sturdy courage and real common sense of the pioneer woman.

She has been a hard worker all her life. In her youth she owned a team of oxen which she drove herself, plowing, clearing, and doing other work which is usually done by strong men.

She fell head over heels in love with young Will York, a blacksmith and hunter, and when her mother and other relatives objected to the match, she eloped with her man across the mountains and married him. After the honeymoon—and this reveals the strong type of woman she was—she returned home to the log cabin, hitched up her oxen, and moved her husband's possessions to a

near-by cabin, where they set up their
home. It must have been a romantic and
beautiful sight to see the young couple
moving—Mother York in her split bonnet
and linsey dress driving the oxen, with her
young husband in jeans, and probably
"toting" a muzzle-loader, tramping along
behind.

Children came in rapid succession,
healthy and mostly red-headed babies—
Henry, Alvin, Sam, George, Joe, Lillie, Jim,
Albert, Robert, and others—eleven of them.
The father sang as he blacksmithed in the
cave which the Long Hunter had discovered over one hundred fifty years ago, or
beamed with happiness as he slipped
through the woods, hunting and shooting.
The little mother remained at home, cooking, keeping house, and bringing up children. It is not hard for us to picture her
in the little mountain cabin with the
puncheon floors and the rough log walls
chinked with clay and bark. She carded
and spun and wove the simple homespun
for the clothes and cooked the meat and
wild game her husband provided, carefully
saving the tallow, with which she made

soap and candles. Somehow or other she also found time to yoke up her oxen and plow and plant potatoes and other vegetables. When business at the blacksmith shop was dull and game was scarce, she hired out to the neighbors and washed and cooked to help earn food and clothes for her family. She loved her children with the wistful and beautiful love of a great mother. She never spoiled them. When, with the mischievousness of growing boys and girls, they overstepped the mark, she quietly and quickly reached for the hickory stick and effectively proved that she was the "boss." Tender and loving as she was, she nevertheless did not believe in sparing the rod and spoiling the child.

Occasionally there were trips to Jamestown, the county seat, with loads of sorghum and other farm produce. Such a journey was always a thrilling adventure. "Jimtown," as the mountaineers called it, was only nine miles away, but the road led up creek beds and over mountain trails and the trip took many, many hours.

To a mountain child a visit to "Jimtown" was something for which one

Mother York, the wonderful pioneer mother of America's most
distinguished soldier

dreamed and planned and lay breathless in
the teeming silence of the mountain night.
How old and important a little boy or girl
felt when he or she was considered old
enough to sit up beside father in the ram-
bling farm wagon and undertake the long
journey to the big town—uphill with the
horses dragging their load desperately,
downhill through mud ruts and dust clouds,
on and on with the limitless sky overhead
and crickets singing beside the winding
road.

Then "Jimtown" at last—its hundreds of
people, its neat houses painted and lined
up on streets, its porches jutting out over
velvety lawns; its general store, its post
office; the hustle and bustle, the laughing,
the trading, the gossiping.

Somehow one did not say much in "Jimtown." It was all so new and dazzling and
there was so much to look at. But what a
tale it made for the smaller children at
home in the rude log cabin on the mountain
side!

When new settlers arrived in the valley,
the mountaineers turned out to help them
with their new home. The men felled the

trees and rolled the logs to one side and helped put in the crop. The women made quilts. These log rollings and quiltings were always bright spots in the life of the little backwoods community. Mother York always took part in them and enjoyed them tremendously. There were the "beeves" and the turkey shoots. The crack shots assembled on the mountain side for a day's shooting. Her husband was one of the greatest of them all, and invariably brought home a turkey gobbler or a portion of beef.

When the blacksmith died, she carried on just the same, and with much mother love, hard work, and occasional applications of the hickory stick, raised her boys and girls to manhood and womanhood.

She has no regrets. She declares she would do it again, and happily too. "I worked so hard I never had time to be unhappy."

She lives with her now grown and married sons and daughters. She visits them in their different cabins and helps and advises them in the raising of their families. On a Sunday, she is usually to be found in the home of her famous soldier son, where the family generally unite. The mountain people are very clannish and are likely to stick together and live near one another. The Yorks are no exception.

Mother York has very little to say about the great fame which has come to her second eldest son, and she rarely comments on it. She is very proud of his World War record and his high place in the national life of his country, but she is even more proud of his fine character, manly bearing, and true Americanism. "What do you think of America's most distinguished soldier?" I inquired, nodding toward Alvin. "He's a purty good son and a tol'able nice husband," she answered.

When I asked her how she liked all this fame and publicity, she smiled wistfully, a dreamy look appeared in her eyes, and she said, "I think I would rather be back in the old days. I had to work mighty hard to bring the eleven of them up, but I did it. I loved it. And I would do it again." She looked around the room at her splendid sons and daughters. "I could handle them then. I always knowed whar they was. But now"—she smiled again—"I guess they've growed up and I ain't so sure of their whereabouts." Everybody laughed happily.

The little old mother in her linsey dress and split bonnet is still the head of the House of York.

## Chapter X

## "Larnin'"

BEFORE the World War there was very little money in the mountains. The soil was arid and, except in the valleys and river bottoms, it was difficult to raise good crops. The grazing was not much better, and the razorbacks and scrub cattle eked out a bare existence. The timber forests were gradually disappearing. Game was not so plentiful as it had been. Markets were far away. Transportation was far behind the times. The main highways were frequently only creek beds and winding trails. People found it more profitable to sell their corn distilled in gallon jars than in sacks and wagonloads. Cabins were often dilapidated and farms backward and run down. Life was a hard and relentless fight with a none too bountiful nature.

The mountaineers living in the "Valley of the Three Forks of the Wolf" and in the coves and back creeks could not possibly have afforded to pay for a school the year around. Had they been able to finance it, the children could not have attended safely and conveniently. The roads were very bad in the winter time, and there were but few bridges across the rapidly rising creeks. Under the circumstances, the school ran in the summer time only. Even then, crops and foddering interfered. The little valley school ran on an average of ten weeks a year. It was a small frame building with one room, one teacher, and a shocking shortage of books and other equipment. The children had to sit on split-peg stools with their feet not even touching the floor.

The nearest passenger railroad was over fifty miles away. The nearest up-to-date school was about the same distance.

To a great extent the appalling ignorance and backwardness of the mountain people was due to the shocking dearth of good schools. The boys and girls simply could not get what they called "larnin'." It was not their fault, but was due to the isolation of the mountain communities, the poor nature of the country, and the bad roads and trails.

Most mountain people were illiterate,
unlearned, and ignorant, but not stupid.
Ignorance is no more a proof of stupidity
than a college diploma is of genius. The
stories and novels which described them as
shiftless "mountain whites," always feuding
and moonshining, were very much over-
drawn and not supported by the facts.
For the last twenty years feuds had been
dying out. Only the more lawless indulged
in moonshining. The great majority were
decent, hard-working, and extremely intelligent men and women. Their aversion to
strangers, "furiners," as they called them,
was not due so much to mistrust and sus-
picion as to a very natural shyness and
reticence common to people who live in
isolated communities. They generally
"toted rifle-guns." This does not mean
that they were out to shoot somebody, or
were afraid of being shot themselves. They
knew that there was always the chance of
scaring up a fox or picking off a squirrel,
or a turkey gobbler, and so they usually
took a gun along with them. It cannot be
overemphasized that their love of firearms
was not due to bloodthirstiness, but merely

to their natural love of hunting and shooting.

Alvin York, along with his brothers and sisters and the other boys and girls in the neighborhood, attended the little valley school. ·Alvin went ten weeks a year for five years and finished with the equivalent of a second-grade education. It is very doubtful whether he could have passed the second grade. Thus, through no fault of his own, but because of the absence of educational facilities, he has to go through life handicapped by illiteracy and a meager education.

His plight is the same as that of hundreds of thousands of decent and intelligent men and women who live in the mountains. In spite of this handicap, he has a nobility of character which only one man in a million has, and is touched with the divine fire of genius.

He really mastered only two books at school—an old-fashioned reader and the life of Jesse James.

Fortunately for him and for others of his type, "book larnin'," as it is called in the mountains, is not the only way to acquire an education. There is another way of "larnin' "—from nature. The birds of the air, the beasts of the field, the little "critters" of the soil, the flowers and trees, the running streams, and the soil itself, all have much to teach the observant. Daniel Boone, David Crockett, Sam Houston, Andrew Jackson, and Abraham Lincoln learned much more from nature than from books. This is not meant to be an argument against education. In all probability, they would have been even greater had they been able to attend up-to-date schools and colleges. Because they were unable to do so, they had to teach themselves as best they could. They did so by studying and observing nature. They made a good job of it. The history of this great country records it.

This is especially true of Sergeant Alvin C. York. He loved the woods, understood and learned from them.

His father, a mighty hunter and a dead shot, trained him to be likewise. He schooled him to observe everything when he was out hunting, to use his eyes, his ears, and his powers of reasoning, to shoot quickly and accurately, to develop and harden his muscles, and to acquire patience.

The hunter's profession is, to say the least, a healthful one. He spends much of his time out of doors, where the air is clean, the water sweet and clear, and the food fresh and wholesome. The years in the forest harden and toughen his body until he is as lithe and sinewy as a panther, with a mind that is always on the alert and wondrously quick at making decisions.

A hunter has to learn to be self-reliant and to depend upon himself and upon himself alone. It is well known that "he who stands alone stands strongest." He has to acquire that patience without which it is impossible to trail foxes and follow the tracks of a bear, or to get within shooting distance of a squirrel or a turkey. He must cultivate stealth and swiftness.

Through years of hunting in the woods, Alvin, the mightiest hunter and the greatest shot in all the mountains, acquired these fundamental things and gradually made them part of his daily life. He is quiet of speech, patient, healthy, self-disciplined, self-reliant, and always in repose until an

occasion calls for him to act.    Then he
acts swiftly, surely, and silently.

He has studied the animals of the forest
until he has learned their ways and their
methods of living.   His language is richly
interspersed with references to them.    In
referring to the two German stretcher
bearers he surprised coming down the path
toward him that morning in the Argonne,
he did not say that he discovered or ran
into them; he merely remarked that he
"flushed" them, just as any hunter would
flush a covey of quail.   When the other
boys leveled their rifles to fire he told them
not to do so: "We will trail them to their
dens and then we will know where their
dens are."   That is the language of the
fox hunter.

I have hunted so much with Alvin York
and listened to so many of his tales and
picturesque dissertations upon the woods
and habits of the animals, that I am fairly
well acquainted with his out-of-doors philosophy of life.

The mountaineers are very fond of wild
honey.   They will go to all sorts of trouble
and submit to terrific punishment to get

the honeycomb.   They lay out a bee bait
of brown sugar, or some other sweet sub-
stance, on the rocks and logs in the mountains and then attempt to follow the bees
to their hive, which is likely to be located
in a tall, hollow tree on the mountain top,
in the most inaccessible part of the forest.
Cutting down one of these trees and getting
the honey is one of the most popular of all
mountain sports.

Some men are not at all afraid of bees,
and, strange to say, not bothered by them.
Henry York will tackle a hive with his
bare hands, his shirt open at the neck, and
no protection whatsoever for his head.   The
bees seldom sting him, and when they do,
he doesn't seem to bother.   Jim York, one
of the youngest of the brothers, is peculiarly
susceptible.   The last time we cut down a
bee tree, he was so badly stung around the
ankles that he could not walk home and
for days was unable to wear his shoes.
I have even seen the hero of the World War
driven out of the woods by a number of
infuriated bees.   Alvin likes the honey, but
has not much use for the makers of it,
and they have even less use for him when

he is around.    Nevertheless, he always goes
with us when we have located a bee tree.

One evening, armed with axes, pails,
gloves, and bee bonnets, we struck out
through the woods after the golden fluid.
Miles deep in the forest, the boys had
located a bee tree, and, according to their
reports, it was a "whopper."

As we strolled along the trail through the
mountains, Alvin indulged in one of his
rare and wonderful discussions of nature
and animals.   He told me that bees are the
hardest-working, fiercest-fighting, most sensible and homelike creatures in the forest.
They go out and do things while other little
creatures on wings fool away their time,
butterflying around and warming themselves in the sun.   Bees know how to save,
too, and when winter comes have a nice,
warm home and plenty of honey to live
on.   They punish and drive out the
idlers, are clean and brave and take wonderful care of their queen.   They bring her the
best honey, defend her with their lives, and
when their hives are attacked, swarm
around and protect and, if possible, hide
her.

As we plodded along over the mountain trail, he compared the bees to human beings and added, "If men and women would only pull together, work hard and save like the bees, they would be much happier." He mentioned the fact that although the bees were very brave and hard fighters, if left alone, they mind their own business and live in peace. They do not want to sting anybody. They lose their lives when they do, because the sting rips out and kills them. They seem to know this, and if you refrain from molesting their home they in turn will not bother you. "Some day," added the big fellow, "nations will learn their philosophy and live in peace, and then we will have a real world." He emphasized and praised the social sense of bees. He admired their intelligence. He told me that if a mouse enters the hive, the bees immediately sting it to death, and then being unable to move it because it is so heavy, they hermetically seal it in wax and so preserve it from decay and from polluting their homes. Suddenly he stopped, threw his head back on his shoulders and laughed the "Ho! ho!" of the mountaineers. He then told me of

a giant moth which enters the hives, spins
a web around itself, and so prevents the
bees from getting at it, and then deliberately
eats the bees out of hive and home. "That
moth," he commented, "is what I call a
genius."

Arriving at the bee tree on top of the
mountain, we slipped off our hunting jackets
and proceeded to fell it. It was a giant
hollow oak. We could see the bees entering through a small opening near the top.
We had to notch the tree so that it would
fall upon a near-by cedar, which would
break the fall and prevent it from smashing
to pieces when it hit the ground, in which
event the honey would be scattered and
lost and the bees probably declare a general
warfare upon us. Our plan of campaign
was to fell the tree against the cedar, and
as it slipped to the ground, rush forward,
plug the hole, and trap the bees. We then
planned to saw off the hollow portion of the
tree which contained the hive.

Alas, the bees had their own idea of all
this! The wood was dry. The chopping
hard. Our shirts, wet with perspiration,
clung to our backs. The bees, believing

that the best defensive is an offensive, angrily attacked us, and soon the forest was reverberating with cries and yells of pain.   Some of us slipped on our gloves and bee bonnets.

In falling, the tree hit the cedar with a glancing blow, ricocheted, and smashed. The next moment we were in the midst of broken branches, maddened bees, and bucketfuls of golden honey.

Our casualties mounted quickly.   Jim and Alvin were the first to be driven out— Jim with swollen ankles and a sting in his tongue which he received when he unwarily bit a piece of comb with an angry bee inside it, and Alvin, according to his own version, with more stings in his hide than a porcupine has quills.   He was soon *hors de combat* and called it a day.   Some bees got inside my bonnet, but luckily I was able to shake them out before they did much damage.   The rest of my armor seemed to be sting-proof, and I was able to stick it out, although when a few bees got to my legs, I began to have serious misgivings.

Old Henry, with bare hands and shirt open at the neck and honey and bees all over him, was having a glorious time. As one of the mountaineers remarked, he was too casehardened to feel pain, and if the bees stung him, they merely bent their stingers.

After we had taken out two buckets full of honey, I began to grow used to it. However, a number of bees found a flaw in my armor and began to make the most of it. I yelled and danced around the log like an Indian on the warpath. I made up my mind, though, to stay until the finish. I shall never forget my relief when the last drops of honey were taken out, and the job seemed to be over. Alas, my consternation, when that bear cat of a Henry began to stir up the bees in an attempt to find the queen! I left and left fast.

We were all pretty badly stung and unanimously agreed that bees were "not much on the pull, but awful mean on the push." We got the honey—and everything that went with it.

The following morning, one of the boys returned with a brand-new beehive which he had made himself. He located the queen, put her inside, and when her loyal subjects swarmed in after her, he sealed the box and brought it home.   The hive is now in his garden.

Fox hunting also appeals strongly to the red-headed sergeant.   He insists that even foxes are very home-loving.   They circle and always return to their dens.   He knows how long the circling takes—for the gray fox about one hour, the red fox anything up to twenty-four hours.   "Most human beings ought to learn to do likewise," he commented.   "Foxes don't work hard though," he added, " like bees.   They are pretty lazy, and so they are being exterminated while the bees are being gradually domesticated."

He regards the mountain cats as the greatest advertisers in the forest.   They are neither very brave, not first-class fighters, but they make such a lot of noise spitting and hissing and snarling that they generally manage to scare off other animals.   "They're right smart advertisers," he concluded with a grin.

Coons are just the opposite.   They can whip a cat any time.   It takes a mighty good dog to beat them.   But they are very

stupid. Once the hounds get on their
trails, instead of circling and doubling and
trying to throw them off the scent as the
foxes do, they generally clamber up a
near-by tree, which is exactly what they
should not do, because then the hounds
have them treed. When the tree is cut
down, they do the most stupid thing.
Instead of jumping clear, they run the full
length of the fallen tree, as if they have
not realized it is down. The hounds wait
at the butt and get them. "That's jes'
plain dumbness," he remarked.

The squirrels command his interest—so
much so that often instead of shooting them
he lies out in the forest, listens to their
chatter, and watches their graceful leaps
from tree to tree and their flights over the
forest. They chatter so much they attract
the attention of the hunter, whereas if they
remained quiet, they would probably be
safe. "Lots of human beings are like that,"
he compared, "they talk too much." The
squirrels collect and save nuts, but they
generally forget where they have stored
them. They haven't nearly as much sense
as the bees.

Often he talks of the days when the mountains and the hollows were full of "ba'ar'." Tales of the "ba'ar" hunts of David Crockett and Daniel Boone come readily from his lips. "They were hunters!" he will add, his eyes gleaming with admiration. Bears are scarce now, and they stay far back in the mountains. Some time ago, Sam, while driving a motor truck into the mountains, was crossing a trestle bridge, when suddenly he saw a bear coming across from the other side. Sam immediately went into reverse, backed up, and gave the bear the right of way. We kidded him over this and asked him why he did not step on the gas and slap the bear. He merely grinned and commented, "You don't know bears." Alvin added, "You can get a bear 'most any day if you hunt hard enough, but motor trucks are most awful scarce down this way."

Sergeant York knows the lights of Broadway and of the other big cities. He does not miss them. He prefers the forests flooded with moonlight, the stars swinging low overhead, and the strange and subtle scents of the trees to all of the city lights

in the world. He would rather listen to
the whippoorwill calling to his mate, or the
mocking bird pouring out its soul in golden
song, than visit all of the theaters and
opera houses in the world.

Most passionately of all he loves the soil,
the rich, brown soil of the little valley
tucked away among the mountains. He
seems to draw strength from it. He commented: "If you have never sat on a
harvester in the early dawn and filled your
lungs with mountain air, perfumed with
the scents of the forest, and seen the beautiful, golden stalks going down under the
blades, you have never really seen anything or been anywhere."

Walking and hunting through the woods,
observing the habits of wild life, never less
lonely than when he was alone, Alvin York
has learned some of the fundamental truths
of life and has found repose and happiness,
and "that peace which passeth all understanding."

## Chapter XI

# Hunting

THE mountaineers have ample opportunity to use their "rifle-guns." There is still a reasonable amount of game left in the woods, red and gray foxes on the mountain side, coons and cats in the hollows; squirrels in the forest, wild turkeys in the valleys, with deer and bear away back in, and quail everywhere.

When Daniel Boone passed through the Cumberland Mountains over a hundred fifty years ago, the whole countryside was so teeming with game that he lingered for several days. He is said to have stood on one of the mountain peaks and exclaimed, "I am richer than the man mentioned in the Scriptures who owned the cattle on a thousand hills; I own the wild beasts of more than a thousand valleys."

The mountaineers cherish the story of how he often leaped on the back of a buffalo and dispatched the beast with his bowie knife.

David Crockett, who died like a man at
the Alamo, never tired of telling in his auto-
biography of the abundance of game in the
mountain country.

"Davy" was one of the greatest hunters
who ever lived, and probably killed more
bear than any other frontiersman.   He
actually killed over one hundred in one
year.   Here is his classic description of a
bear fight at night:

The woods were very rough and hilly, and all
covered over with cane.

I now was compelled to move on more slowly;
and was frequently falling over logs, and into the
cracks made by the earthquakes, so that I was very
much afraid I would break my gun.   However, I
went on about three miles, when I came to a good,
high creek, which I waded.   It was very cold and
the creek was about knee-deep; but I felt no great
inconvenience from it just then, as I was all over
wet with sweat from running, and I felt hot enough.
After I got over this creek and out of the cane,
which was very thick on all our creeks, I listened
for my dogs.   I found they had either treed or
brought the bear to a stop, as they continued barking in the same place.   I pushed on as near in the
direction of the noise as I could, till I found the
hill was too steep for me to climb, and so I backed
and went down the hill some distance, till I came

to a hollow, and then took up that, till I came to a place where I could climb up the hill. It was mighty dark and was difficult to see my way or anything else. When I got up the hill, I found I had passed the dogs; and so I turned and went to them. I found when I got there, they had treed the bear in a large forked poplar, and it was sitting in the fork.

I could see the lump, but not plain enough to shoot with any certainty, as there was no moonlight; and so I set in to hunting for some dry brush to make me a light; but I could find none, though I could find that the ground was torn mightily to pieces by the cracks.

At last I thought I could shoot by guess, and kill him; so I pointed as near the lump as I could, and fired away. But the bear didn't come, he only clumb up higher and got on a limb, which helped me to see him better. I now loaded up again and fired, but this time he didn't move at all. I commenced loading for a third fire, but the first thing I knowed the bear was down among my dogs, and they were fighting all around me. I had my big butcher knife in my belt, and I had a pair of dressed buckskin breeches on. So I took out my knife and stood, determined, if he should get hold of me, to defend myself in the best way I could.

I stood there for some time, and could now and then see a white dog which I had, but all the rest of them, and the bear, which was dark-colored, I couldn't see at all, it was so miserable dark. They still fought around me, and sometimes within three

Typical mountain school before the World War

feet; but at last the bear got down into one of the cracks that the earthquake had made in the ground, about four feet deep, and I could tell the biting end of him by the hollering of my dogs. So I took my gun and pushed the muzzle of it about, till I thought I had it against the main part of his body, and fired; but it happened to be only the fleshy part of his foreleg. With this he jumped out of the crack, and he and the dogs had another hard fight around me, as before. At last, however, they forced him back into the crack again, as he was when I had shot.

I had laid down my gun in the dark, and now I began to hunt for it; and while hunting, I got hold of a pole, and I concluded I would punch him a while with that. I did so, and when I would punch him, the dogs would jump in on him, when he would bite them badly, and they would jump out again. I concluded as he would take punching so patiently it might be that he would lie still enough for me to get down in the crack, and feel slowly along until I could find the right place to give him a dig with the butcher. So I got down and my dogs got in before him and kept his head towards them, till I got along easily up to him; and placing my hand on his rump felt for his shoulder, just behind which I intended to stick him. I made a lunge with my long knife, and fortunately stuck him right through the heart, at which he just sank down, and I crawled out in a hurry. In a little time my dogs all come out too, and seemed satisfied, which was the way they always had of telling me they had finished him.

I suffered very much that night with cold, as my leather breeches and everything else I had on, was wet and frozen.   But I managed to get my bear out of his crack after several hard trials and so I butchered him and laid down to try to sleep.   But my fire was very bad, and I couldn't find anything that would burn well to make it any better; and so I concluded I should freeze, if I didn't warm myself in some way by exercise.   So I got up and hollered a while, and then I would just jump up and down with all my might, and throw myself into all sorts of motions.   But all of this wouldn't do, for my blood was now getting cold, and the chills coming all over me.   I was so tired, too, that I could hardly walk; but I thought I would do the best I could to save my life, and then, if I died, nobody would be to blame.   So I went to a tree about two feet through and not a limb on it for thirty feet, and I would climb up to the limbs and lock my arms together around it, and slide down to the bottom again.   This would make the insides of my legs and arms feel mighty warm and good.   I continued this till daylight in the morning, and how often I clumb up my tree and slid down I don't know, but I reckon at least a hundred times.

In the morning I got my bear hung up so as to be safe, and then set out to hunt for my camp.

Poor, isolated, and without much chance to "get larnin'," a great number of the mountaineers, until very recently, were unable to read or write. Histories meant nothing to them. Consequently, they treasured and told and retold the stories that have been handed down from generation to generation. In the mountain stores, around blacksmith shops, at the shooting matches, and in front of the open fire which blazes on winter nights in almost every log cabin, they talked about the hunting and shooting achievements of the pioneers. Davy Crockett's exploits always fascinated them. His "rifle-gun," which he called "Old Betsey," was as well known to them as their own muzzle-loaders. Daniel Boone, too, tremendously appealed to their imagination, and stories of big Sam Houston and Old Hickory whiled away many a long winter night.

Almost every mountaineer is familiar with Davy Crockett's fight with a cougar in Texas:

Night was fast coming on, and as I began to think that I had had just about sport enough for one day, I might as well look around for a place of shelter for the night, and take a fresh start in the morning, by which time I was in hopes my horse would be recruited. Near the margin of the river a large tree had been blown down, and I thought of making my lair in its top, and approached it for that purpose.   While beating among the branches I heard a low growl as much as to say, "Stranger, the apartments are already taken."   Looking about to see what sort of bedfellow I was likely to have, I discovered, not more than five or six paces from me, an enormous Mexican cougar, eying me as an epicure surveys the table before he selects his dish, for I have no doubt the cougar looked upon me as the subject of a future supper.   Rays of light darted from his large eyes, he showed his teeth like a negro in hysterics, and he was crouching on his haunches ready for a spring; all of which convinced me that unless I was pretty quick upon the trigger, posterity would know little of the termination of my eventful career, and it would be far less glorious and useful than I intend to make it.

One glance satisfied me that there was no time to be lost, as Pat thought when falling from a church steeple and exclaimed, "this would be mighty pleasant now if it would only last."   But there was no retreat either for me or the cougar.   So I leveled my Betsey and blazed away.   The report was followed by a furious growl (which is sometimes the case in Congress) and the next moment when I expected to find the tarnal critter struggling with death, I beheld him shaking his head as if nothing more than a bee had stung him.   The ball had struck him on the forehead and glanced off, doing no other injury than stunning him for an instant

and tearing off the skin, which tended to infuriate
him more.

The cougar wasn't long making up his mind what
to do; nor was I neither, but he would have it all
his own way, and vetoes my motion to back out.
I had not retreated three steps before he sprang at
me like a steamboat; I stepped aside, and as he
lit upon the ground, I struck him violently with the
barrel of my rifle, but he didn't mind that but
wheeled around and made at me again.   The gun
was now of no use, so I threw it away, and drew my
hunting knife, for I knew we should come to close
quarters before the fight would be over.   This time
he succeeded in fastening on my left arm, and was
just beginning to amuse himself by tearing the flesh
off with his fangs, when I ripped my knife into his
side, and he let go his hold, much to my satisfaction.

He wheeled about and came at me with increased
fury, occasioned by the smarting of his wounds.   I
now tried to blind him, knowing that if I succeeded
he would become an easy prey, so as he approached
me I watched my opportunity, and aimed a blow at
his eyes with my knife, but unfortunately it struck
him on the nose, and he paid no other attention to
it than by a shake of the head and a low growl.
He pressed me close and as I was stepping backward
my foot tripped in a vine and I fell to the ground.
He was down upon me like a night hawk upon a
June bug.   He seized hold of the outer part of my
right thigh, which afforded him considerable amusement; the hinder part of his body was towards my

face; I grasped his tail with my left hand, and
tickled his ribs with my hunting knife which I held
in my right.

Still the critter wouldn't let go his hold; and as
I found that he would lacerate my leg dreadfully,
unless he was speedily shaken off, I tried to hurl
him down the bank into the river, for our scuffle
had already brought us to the edge of the bank.
I stuck my knife into his side and summoned all my
strength to throw him over.    He resisted, was
desperate heavy; but at last I got him so far down
the declivity that he lost his balance and he rolled
over and over till he landed on the margin of the
river, but in his fall he dragged me along with him.
Fortunately I fell uppermost and his neck presented
a fair mark for my hunting knife.    Without allow-
ing myself time even for drawing my breath, I aimed
one desperate blow at his neck, and the knife entered
his gullet up to the handle, and reached his heart.
He struggled for a few moments and died.    I have
had many fights with bears, but that was mere
child's play; this was the first fight ever I had with
a cougar, and I hope it may be the last.

The mountaineers have an uncanny sense
of direction.    They can plunge into the
most isolated cove, and, after hunting
squirrel or foxes for days, can immediately
turn around and go home in a bee line.
They love the woods, the fragrance, the
stillness, and the loneliness.    They never

tire of discussing the three months Daniel
Boone spent alone in the forest in what we
now call Kentucky.  The nearest settlement
was hundreds of miles away.  He had not
even a dog nor a horse with him.  He had
no bread, no salt, no sugar.  Every few
days he had to change his camp in order to
throw the Indians off his trail.  He probably wandered hundreds of miles.  Nevertheless, he met his brother, returning from
North Carolina, at the exact hour and
place they had agreed upon months before.

Brought up on such tales, trained to
handle a gun from childhood, out in the
woods hunting almost as soon as they are
able to toddle, they have grown to love the
out of doors and to achieve much skill in
stalking, trailing, and bringing down game.

Hunting is almost a business with them.
A red fox or coon pelt brings several dollars.
Squirrel pie is regarded as a favorite dish.
Turkey gobblers make excellent victuals.
Deer and bear meat are a great relief from
corn pone and "sow belly," which is almost
their staple meal.

The mountaineers take excellent care of
their "rifle-guns."  They know how to use

them, and have a natural crook under their arms for their stocks.

They are almost as interested in their dogs. They know that a good one helps considerably in trailing foxes, treeing coons, and locating squirrels.

Sergeant York has a couple of "red-bones" and two English walkers. His love for them is equaled only by theirs for him. "Red-bones" are fox hounds. They will not yelp for anything but foxes. Once they get the scent, they will follow until they get the animals or den them. One of them once trailed a fox for forty hours without stopping, and when he returned home, although hardly able to stand, limped over to the big sergeant, wagged his tail, and looked up at him for approval. The English walkers are good all-around dogs, and are used for squirrels, coons, foxes, razor-backs, and even rabbits. The sergeant also has a coon dog, which he refers to as the "coon-treeinest dog you ever seed." A dog has to be a good one to whip a coon.

Next to having a dependable rifle and a dog, the most important thing is that the

Woodrow Wilson York bringing home a turkey shot by his famous father

hunter knows the right kind of clothes to wear. You cannot hunt all day and shoot accurately unless you are comfortable. Clothes which will not turn the water, leggings which will not resist a prickly undergrowth, and boots which are too large or too small will do more to ruin a good hunt than anything else.

Sergeant York generally wears overalls and a coat made of waterproof ducking, with light leggings, hobnail boots, and a broad-brimmed shade hat. Thus outfitted, with the old "rifle-gun" of his ancestors, and "them thar hound-dogs of mine," he is ready for the woods.

The dogs are turned loose and immediately lope out in long circles, sniffing to pick up the scent. If it is a fox, they yelp and immediately give chase. The hunters know by the sound of the yelping how old or new the trail is. If they consider it is new enough, they immediately hurry to some near-by hill where they can get a good look at the countryside. Foxes always circle, and once the hunters gain the radius of the circle they are usually able to intercept it on the return.

Squirrels, if possible, are "barked"; that is, killed by concussion instead of by a direct hit. The big, round ball of the muzzle-loader ruins them when it smashes through them. And so the skilled hunter prefers to hit directly under their heads, almost grazing them. The concussion hurls them lifeless from the trees. Daniel Boone was an expert at this sort of shooting and astounded Audubon, the famous naturalist, with his squirrel barking.

Coons are hunted at night. They generally frequent the hollows and search for nuts, or sometimes raid a near-by corn or potato patch. The dogs give voice as soon as they pick up the scent, and the frightened coon dashes off into the forest with the hounds hot on its trail and the hunters following. When too closely pressed, the coon clambers up a convenient tree. The hunters either have to shoot or shake it out. Sometimes they have to chop the tree down. If the night is dark, they can generally locate the coon's eyes with their flash lights. Failing this, they sometimes have to sleep out under the trees all night, their hounds keeping watch.

Belling hogs is another favorite sport. Turned out in the coves and valleys to fatten on the nuts and berries which abound there, they soon increase and multiply. Every spring the owners have to round them up and attach bells to their necks so that they may know where they are. The dogs quickly take up the trail and bay them. Whereupon, a dog especially trained for the job, usually a mixture of hound and bulldog, seizes the hog by the nose and holds him until the bell is fastened by a strap around the neck. Hogs are fairly savage. When frightened, they always provide much excitement and not a little danger.

CHAPTER XII

## "Beeves" and Turkey Shoots

MENTION has been made of the fact
that when Ferguson, the leader of
the English redcoats at the Battle of King's
Mountain, sent his sneering threat to the
backwoods men, some of them at the time
were actually participating in a turkey
shoot.

These turkey shoots are among the oldest
and most popular of all the mountain sports.
The mountaineers would rather shoot than
eat. The moment turkeys, and for that
matter, "beeves," are mentioned, they
simply abandon whatever they are doing
and start out for the shooting grounds.
I have attended many of these shoots,
shooting, and sometimes acting as one of
the judges.

Davy Crockett was very fond of these
matches, and his old muzzle-loader, which
he affectionately called "Betsey," was, to
use a mountain expression, "pint-blank

sartain death for turkeys." Alvin York's father is still remembered as one of the best match shooters of all times. It remained for the son, however, to prove himself to be the greatest shot that ever squinted down the long barrel of a muzzle-loader and "busted" a turkey gobbler's head.

Recently I participated in one of the biggest turkey shoots and "beeves" ever held in the mountains. The match was held in a rocky field on Sergeant York's farm in the Valley of the Three Forks of the Wolf. Two automobile loads of turkeys and a fat steer were the prizes. Despite the fact that the match was not advertised at all and was hurriedly arranged almost overnight, the best shots in the mountains were on the grounds shortly after sunup. How they found out that we were going to hold a shoot is beyond me. They certainly know how to circulate news in the mountains. The blacksmith shops, post office, and stores seem to be the clearing houses for news of everything that is happening.

John Conatzer was there. He is a typical hill billy, with patches on the knees of his

10

jeans, the most dilapidated old slouch felt hat ever worn, powderhorn and shot pouch slung from his shoulders, and a long muzzle-loading rifle which was used at King's Mountain. John comes from away back in the mountains where the slopes are so steep that you have to wear hobnails in the seat of your breeches in order to get down. His friendly rival, another typical mountaineer, and a great shot, John Souders, was on the ground early. He brought along a muzzle-loader which stood over six feet, an old Decherd flintlock which was down at New Orleans with Old Hickory's men. Ike Hatfield, tall, rangy, and taciturn, and young Oliver Delk were among those present.

They came from the mountains and the foothills, from the coves and the valleys, from the back creeks and the villages; in jeans, overalls, and all sorts of rough hunting and shooting clothes. They came in automobiles, on mules and horseback, and on foot. They "toted" muzzle-loaders.

There they were, the Southern mountaineers, most of them red-headed and raw-boned, and all of them quiet, unassuming, and keen-eyed.    Throughout all of the shooting, I never heard a single dispute over the judges' decisions.    There was no smoking or drinking and  practically no cursing.    Yet these were the supposedly ignorant, feuding, moonshining mountain whites.

All the York boys were there, Alvin conspicuous among them.    He was favored to win and declared he "jes' knowed he was goin' to eat meat."

First the turkeys were tied by a ten-foot string to a stake.    The shooters had to shoot from a standing position two hundred yards away.    The first turkey was a big gobbler.    He held his head high, spread his wings, and preened himself in the glistening sunlight.    He was a big fellow, but two hundred yards is a long distance for these old-fashioned  muzzle-loaders  to  carry. Nevertheless, they did carry, and with deadly effect.

Later on in the morning, the turkeys were moved closer in and tied up behind logs or stones, with only the weaving, bobbing head visible.    This time they were shot from a standing position sixty yards away. The turkey had to be hit between the beak and the gills. It could put its head up or down, weave or bob, or do anything else it liked.

The big red-headed sergeant was first man up. He sighted very carefully, fired, and shot a turkey right through the head. It never even knew what hit it. The next ten shooters killed six turkeys—seven turkeys with eleven shots. That was probably the best shooting ever done in the mountains.

Usually the shooters pay ten cents a shot, the owner, of course, getting the money. If several shooters fire and miss, he is likely to make a good profit, but if the first few men up kill turkeys, he is out of pocket. Nobody ever makes any money when Alvin York draws a fine bead on a turkey's head. Certainly the owners were out of luck on this occasion. I have never seen such shooting. I suppose I never shall again. The sergeant bagged three turkeys, including the thirty-pound gobbler which was the cynosure of all eyes.

In the afternoon the "beeve" began. "Beeve," of course, is old Anglo-Saxon for

The sergeant bagged three turkeys

beef, and a beef, the world over, is a steer.
This one was fattened and ready for the
market and valued at seventy-five dollars.

Shots are usually a dollar each. You
can buy as many as you want to, but you
pay a dollar a shot. The owner gets the
money, in return for which he slaughters,
dresses, and divides the steer. The first
two prizes are the choicest meat, the hind
quarters; the second two, fore quarters;
and the fifth prize, the hide and tallow.

The targets are the most difficult imaginable. Each shooter has an individual
board, across which the referee slashes a
crisscross with a sharp hunting knife. The
center of the crisscross is the bull's-eye.
The shooting is so accurate that if you
want to "taste meat" you have to drive the
center every shot. The distances are forty
yards prone, and twenty-six yards offhand
or standing up. Not even the eagle-eyed
mountaineer can see the bull's-eye from
such distances. He has to use a piece of
white paper or a mark either above or
below, or at one side of the center, to guide
him. The competition is so keen and the
shooting so accurate that often the judges

have to use compasses to determine the winner.

Sergeant Alvin York has been known to buy five shots, fire five times, and drive the steer home alive on the hoof. He very nearly did this at the recent shoot. He won four of the five parts. Doctor Sloan, from Jamestown, after three bad shots, which were wide of the mark, placed one very close to the center, and deprived Alvin of again driving the steer home alive.

The shoots are not without their humorous side. Two years ago when I was down in Tennessee, Sam York "busted" a turkey's head. He threw it down on the ground near where he was standing, and while he was smacking his lips and gleefully telling his friends of the wonderful supper he was going to have, a razorback stole down the mountain side, seized and ran off with the turkey. When Sam discovered his loss, he hollered like a "ba'ar" and chased the hog. The last we saw of them they were going down in a heap, with the turkey and the hog and Sam all mixed up together.

Sometimes the turkey tied to the stake breaks loose and the shooters have to throw down their guns and give chase. Chasing an active turkey up a mountain side is exciting and strenuous. Sometimes a gobbler tied behind a log or stone puts his head down and calmly goes to sleep. Then there is much fun at the expense of the shooter. He has to stand ready while somebody tries to stir up the turkey.

Alvin's bag for the day was three turkeys, including the thirty-pound gobbler, four out of five of the best shots for the beef, and first prize for the best match shooting; that is, for the best consistent shooting of the day. The red-headed mountaineer and doughboy who brought down twenty-eight Germans with twenty-eight shots in the Argonne and who is recognized as the outstanding hero of the World War is still the greatest shot in the mountains.

## Chapter XIII

## The First Fight

AFTER his father died in 1911, Alvin went all to pieces. He was at the age when a certain type of boy thinks it is smart to gamble, curse, and make all sorts of mischief for himself and his friends. He was what the mountaineers called "hog-wild." That explains itself. Worse than that, he was a "hell buster," gambling, drinking, cursing, carrying a pistol and a knife.

It was a difficult task to collect the facts of this rather dark period of his youth. He would not discuss it himself. The more I questioned the more he smiled and remained silent. The other mountaineers at first refused to enlighten me. At any time they are shy, suspicious, and loyal. When I asked about Alvin, they were doubly so. They seemed to sense that he wanted to cover up those days when he sowed enough wild oats to fill the storehouses of Abraham.

They simply would not talk. I did not
know what to do. I knew that Alvin had
lived a wild youth. I wanted to tell the
truth about it, the whole truth and nothing
but the truth, but I could not get any first-
hand information. Finally, I cornered one
of the sergeant's "hog-wild" companions,
Everett Delk. He told me the whole story.
Poor Everett is dead now. He was shot
in a drunken brawl outside of Jamestown
only a few months ago.

I shall never forget the look on the big
fellow's face when I told him that I had
the whole story. He looked surprised and
very much concerned when he inquired,
"What did Everett tell you?"

"Everything," I answered.

He scratched his head for a moment,
grinned and commented, "I'll bet it was a
God's plenty." That was the only time
that he has ever used a byword, let alone
a curse word, in the last fifteen years.

Before the war the Tennessee-Kentucky
border line was a tough place, with
moonshine stills, "blind tigers," saloons,
gambling halls, and dance halls every few
miles.

Alvin stood over six feet, weighed over one hundred eighty pounds, and was red-headed. Hunting and blacksmithing had made him as tough and hard as tempered steel. When he had "guzzled" a quart or so of that raw and fiery Tennessee moonshine and was "rarin' to go," he was a mean man to meet in a brawl or a knife fight.

He frequently "liquored up" and was often drunk. He openly boasted that he could outdrink any other mountaineer along the border line. He thought nothing of swallowing a quart of hard liquor at one sitting. And that Tennessee moonshine— "mountain dew" they called it—is clear and potent. Often he and his companions would have terrific drinking bouts. Each one of them supplied a quart of apple brandy and a quart of moonshine whiskey. They drank as long as they could stand up, but once they fell over, they were disqualified. The one who remained on his feet longest (and it was invariably Alvin) won first prize, which consisted of all the remaining liquor. They used to buy the stuff at Bald Rock or Caney Creek along the border line.

Everett Delk, Marion Leffew, Marion Delk, Henry and Albert York were Alvin's companions in these drunken sprees.

The grand jury got after some of them, and they had to slip across the Kentucky line until the excitement died down. Alvin always "toted" a pistol, which he most certainly knew how to use. More quickly than the eye could follow, he could flip it out and with either hand, from any angle, hit objects at almost inconceivable distances. Jesse James, whose career the big fellow greatly admired in those "hog-wild" days, would have been out of luck had he ever been foolish enough to exchange shots with this dead-shooting blacksmith's son. He never actually shot anybody, but more than once he whizzed a few bullets past an opponent's ear or knocked up the dust around his feet. He usually confined his shooting when he was full of liquor to the geese and turkeys of friendly neighbors.

One dark night, with Everett Delk behind him, he was riding his mule back from Kentucky. Passing over a bridge, his keen eye detected something white in the darkness

below.   He was just drunk and full of
devilment enough to pump a few bullets
into it.   Everett went down to investigate.
He heard a squawking in the water, found
feathers all over the place, and eventually
located a dead goose.

On another occasion he was riding home
on his mule, drunk as usual, and wanting
to shoot things up.   Passing a farmhouse
in the dim light of dawn, he saw a number
of turkey gobblers sitting along the fence.
His eyes gleamed.   His fingers twitched to
pull the trigger.   He could not resist.   At
full gallop, drunk, and in the uncertain
light of early dawn, he flipped out his pistol,
shot six times in rapid succession, and
"busted" the heads of six turkeys.   Shortly
after this, he was arrested for carrying a
weapon.   He pleaded his own case and got
off.

The mountaineers still talk of his extraordinary skill with a pistol.   He could even
toss it from hand to hand, and at full gallop,
shoot with deadly accuracy.   Only recently
he sat in a chair on the front veranda of
his home and shot off a crow's head over
one hundred eighty yards away.

Alvin took his mother in his arms and promised her he would abandon
the old life forever

He was almost as good with a knife. He once entered a church and pulled one of his enemies with whom he had had an argument over a girl, out of a pew, dragged him outside, and probably would have cut him up had friends not intervened.

Everett told a story of how the two of them were so full of liquor one night that they fell off their mules. Everett somehow or other managed to get on his feet again, but Alvin was sprawled flat on his face—out. Everett desperately tried to arouse him. In vain. In his befuddled brain, he remembered reading somewhere that the best way to arouse a drunken man is to give him a sudden shock. Suiting the action to the word, he tore a paling off a near-by fence, stood over Alvin, and, swinging the paling like a baseball bat, slapped Alvin where he felt it most. The big fellow, thinking somebody was after him, roared like a "ba'ar," jumped up, swiftly mounted his mule, and rode off through the trees like an express train.

He usually gambled his wages away every week-end at poker, dice, or some other game of chance.

His vocabulary of "cuss" words was a lengthy one, and it is said that he could curse for five minutes without using the same word twice.

On the first of January, 1915, he gained one of the greatest victories a man can hope to achieve. He conquered himself. He came home one night, drunk as usual, and found his little mother sitting up waiting for him. When he asked her why she had not gone to bed, she sobbed and told him that she knew he was out drinking and fighting; that she knew how big and strong and wild he was; and that she was always afraid something would happen to him. She said that she could not go to sleep until she knew he was safe at home. That stung him. It also brought to the surface everything that was fine and manly in his character. He took her in his arms and solemnly promised that he would never drink, gamble, fight, smoke, use a single "cuss" word, lose his temper, or raise his voice in angry heat again as long as he lived.

From that day to this—and that was more than fifteen years ago—he has never backslidden. He fought through the World War without once whiffing a cigarette or slipping back to an *estaminet*\* to sup *vin rouge*. He has never since gambled in any shape or form. He has never lost his temper. Although I have known him for years, I have never known him to use a single curse word, or even to raise his voice in anger. He has abandoned the old life completely and forever.

It was a hard struggle at first, especially on Saturday night, when his "hog-wild" companions invited him to go with them to Kentucky and whoop things up. But he won out. Very recently he told me that "smoking and drinking was most awful unnecessary."

In his middle twenties, Alvin York had learned one of the fundamental lessons of life—before you can hope to conquer other people you must conquer yourself. In the expressive language of the mountaineer, "He done done it."

As his biographer, I wanted to know what greater inner awakening had occurred to inspire him to make this tremendous change

---

\* A café where smoking is permitted and wines are sold.

in his mode of living. He told me of the incident with his mother, which I have described; of a fire-and-brimstone evangelist who had "frightened the devil out of him"; and, shyly, of a beautiful mountain girl named Gracie Williams, whom he truly loved, and who would have nothing to do with him while he was a wild man. At last he told the real reason, the dominating factor. Again I quote his exact words, "I abandoned the old life completely and forever, because I jes' kinder realized I was missing the finer things of life; and when you miss the finer things of life, you might jes' as well be a razorback hog grubbing for acorns on the mountain side." If every boy and girl, and for that matter, every man and women in the world, would only take that advice, "*If you miss the finer things of life, you may as well be a razorback hog grubbing for acorns on the mountain side,*" what a wonderful world we should have!

He went from one extreme to the other and from being a "hell buster" he became a "heaven raiser"—a Sunday-school teacher and a singing elder in the valley church.

## CHAPTER XIV

# War

DURING the early days of the World War Alvin York was blacksmithing and hunting in the little valley. His "hog-wild" days were left behind forever. He was, to use his own expression, "saved." He worked hard at his trade each day and saved a little money; and at night tramped the hills and hollows, hunting for coons and possums. Every Sunday he conducted a children's Sunday-school class in the little valley church and afterwards led the congregation in singing. He had a natural tenor voice which he improved by taking lessons at Byrdstown. He was becoming known now as the Singing Elder.

He was in love, helplessly and hopelessly in love, with Gracie Williams, a mountain girl with blue laughing eyes and chestnut-brown hair. She was one of the mountain belles—young, beautiful, and as shy as a fawn. She had frowned upon Alvin's

11

(147)

drinking and gambling, but now that he was
leading a decent life, she was more inclined
to smile in his direction.

Her parents were opposed to the match
and in fact forbade her seeing him. However, there was a winding lane which dipped
out of sight behind the hills. It was lined
with honeysuckle and shaded with big
trees. The Wolf River sang merrily near
by. It was an ideal place for lovers. In
the late afternoon when the blue hills were
dissolving in gray and the shadows were
stealing over the valley, Alvin used to
whistle to his hound dogs, shoulder his
muzzle-loader, and go up the lane, looking
for squirrel. It generally happened that at
about the same time Gracie was passing
that way, looking for the cows. Thus the
courtship progressed. Alvin gently but
firmly pressed her to name the day. She
just as gently but firmly declined. The big
fellow was worried. According to his own
version he was "pestered a plenty." Often
at nighttime, he would go out on the mountain side, sit down on a log, and gaze
yearningly across the valley to where the
lights flickered in Gracie's home.

Suddenly, the war broke out of a clear blue sky. At first, Alvin, like most of the mountaineers, was only mildly interested. Germany was so far away that he had but the haziest ideas of exactly where it was. If the European powers wanted to fight and "muss each other up," it was none of his business. Even later, when America came in on the side of the Allies, he was not very much concerned. He was at heart a pacifist with a longing for peace. He had tried that fighting business along the Tennessee-Kentucky line and had turned his back on it forever, because he had found that it "didn't profit a man nohow." He wanted to live and let live. He was not interested in the outside world. The war meant nothing to him.

A few weeks later, when Gracie said yes and allowed him to name the day, the war meant even less. Let others fight. He preferred to live in peace and to love and to be loved; to marry Gracie and settle down in the little valley, where for over one hundred fifty years his people had made their homes and lived and loved and worked and hunted. He smiled as he worked at his blacksmith trade, and whistled merrily when he arose at dawn and tramped out over the hills with his hound dogs following. The old desire to drink and gamble and fool around had left him forever. He had found comfort in religion and happiness in love.

If the world would only let him alone, he would be well content in turn to let the world alone. He most surely had no intention of volunteering for active service. The war meant nothing to him. He had no idea what the fighting was about.

Then one evening he received through the mail a little red card instructing him to register for the draft. He filled out the registration card and wrote across the bottom of it, "I don't want to fight."

## CHAPTER XV

## Conscientious Objector

IN the archives of the War Department in Washington, D. C., is a little official slip of paper, marked "Alvin Cullum York, Conscientious Objector."

The Singing Elder in the little valley church, and the man of peace, had been drafted for active service. He could not believe it. After struggling so hard to abandon his "hog-wild" habits, he had conquered and was leading a good Christian life. Through his religion and his love for Gracie, he was for the first time really enjoying happiness, and now his country wanted him to abandon all of this and go to war and fight and kill. He was not going to do it, and immediately claimed exemption.

I have copied the following documents from the official records in the archives of the War Department in Washington:

August 28, 1917

To Local Draft Board,
County of Fentress.

I, Alvin Cullum York, Serial Number 378, hereby certify that I am 29 years of age and reside at Pall Mall, Tennessee.

I hereby respectfully claim discharge from selective draft on the following ground, that I am—

(1) a person who was a member of a well-recognized sect or organization, organized and existing May 18, 1917, whose then existing creed or principles forbade its members to participate in war in any form and whose religious principles are against war or participation therein in accordance with the creed or principles of said well-recognized sect or organization.

The local draft board, however, thought differently about York's religious principles against war. They knew that Alvin York was a big strong fellow, a dead shot, and the type of man who ought to make a good soldier. They knew, too, that he had been "hog wild." They denied his appeal for exemption. Here is their reply, taken from the records in the War Department:

LOCAL BOARD FOR THE COUNTY OF
FENTRESS
STATE OF TENNESSEE
JAMESTOWN, TENNESSEE

Serial Number 378                    Order N. 218

ALVIN CULLUM YORK

Denied, because we do not think "The Church of Christ in Christian Union" is a well-recognized religious sect, etc.  Also, we understand it has no creed except the Bible, which its members more or less interpret for themselves, and some do not disbelieve in war—at least there is nothing forbidding them to participate.

Alvin immediately appealed against their decision, and, when they denied his appeal, went over the heads of the County Board, and armed with affidavits swearing that his religion was opposed to war and fighting, petitioned the Board for the Middle District of Tennessee to exempt him.  When they in turn refused his petition and ordered him to camp, he sat down in the little log cabin, and in the dim light of a kerosene lamp, with paper and pencil, slowly and painfully wrote a personal appeal to Woodrow Wilson himself.  He told the President that he was a poor mountain boy and a lover of peace who did not want to fight or kill anybody, and would not the President allow him to remain at home?

President Wilson turned this wondrously human letter over to the War Department, where it was not acted upon, and later put away in the archives.

Alvin York had to go to war.  Thus, strange as it seems, the man who was destined to become the outstanding hero of the World War was not a regular army man, nor a volunteer.  He was not the killer type.  He was not even the fighting type.  He had no stomach for the business. He was a man of peace, and thrice a conscientious objector.  He went to war because he was forced to go.  He was drafted.

The official records in Washington show that when he was physically examined at Jamestown he weighed over one hundred eighty pounds, stood over six feet tall, and was a perfect specimen of physical manhood.  Hunting and blacksmithing had toughened and hardened his body until he was a man of steel and hickory.  His movements were quiet, quick, and panther-like.

He "toted" his suit case and walked out of the mountains alone.   Upon his return eighteen months later he was greeted by over fifty thousand mountaineers.   The whole nation knew him.   His name was a household word.

## CHAPTER XVI

## Camp

ALVIN YORK caught the train fifty miles away, at Oneida, Tennessee, and immediately started for Camp Gordon, which was situated outside of Atlanta, Georgia, where he was later attached, as a private, to the 82d Division.

This division was made up of units from almost all over America—cow-punchers from Oklahoma, ranchers from the Panhandle in Texas, fruit growers from California, lumbermen from Oregon, farmers from the Middle West, anthracite coal miners from Pennsylvania, mill hands from the industrial centers of New England, mountaineers from Appalachia, cotton growers from the South, and street-bred youths from New York and Brooklyn. It was a perfect cross section of American life and was similar to the Rainbow Division in that it embraced almost all states and all American racial strains. It was appropriately named the All-American Division.

In February, 1918, Alvin was attached to Company G of the 328th Battalion of this division. His company commander was Captain E. C. B. Danforth, Jr., from Augusta, Georgia, and his battalion officer was Major George Edward Buxton, a Plattsburg man, a friend of Theodore Roosevelt, and a blue-blooded New Englander from Providence, Rhode Island. In the mountaineer's company were Greeks, Poles, Italians, Irishmen, East Side Jews, and some American-born boys. Almost half of them were unable to read or write, and a number could not even speak the English language. They were a rough, tough lot, and did their share of boozing, gambling, leave breaking, and whooping things up. They were good soldiers, loyal companions, and they were later to prove, at Saint-Mihiel and in the Argonne, as recklessly brave and fearless a company as ever crossed the seas.

At first the Singing Elder, with his hymns, Bible, and abhorrence of drinking, gambling, and fighting, was out of his ele-

ment.   Besides, he had never met foreign-
born boys.   His knowledge of human beings
was strictly limited to the pure Anglo-
Saxon type on the mountains.   There were
no other racial strains there at all.   There
was not even a colored man back where he
came from.   Like most mountaineers, he
regarded and referred to everybody outside
of the mountain country as "furiners."
No wonder that he wrote in his little diary,
"I am the homesickest boy you ever seed."

However, he was a good soldier, intelligent, conscientious, diligent, and amenable
to discipline, and he quickly won the notice
and respect of his superiors.   His captain
would have liked very much to have promoted him to be a corporal and possibly a
sergeant, but the cloud of conscientious
objector hovered over him.   He remained
a private.   At first he was detailed to
kitchen police, picking up cigar stubs and
papers and cleaning up the lines.   He did
squads right and squads left, learned to
shoulder and present arms, and went on
long route marches.

A few days after he entered camp, he
wrote home: "They done give me a dirty,

greasy old army rifle, and tomorrow they
are a-goin' to take me out on the rifle range
to teach me how to shoot. Ho! ho!"

He missed his old muzzle-loader. He
had grown up with it, had always kept it
clean and in good order, and understood it
and cared for it as if it had been a living
thing. The new service rifle was very
strange to him. Soon, however, he learned
to appreciate it. A few days later he wrote
home again: "They done takened me out
on the rifle ranges to teach me how to
shoot. Them thar boys in my outfit not
only missed the targets, but they missed
the hills on which we put the targets."

Alvin was still thinking in terms of guns
and shooting and was still inclined to judge
men more or less by their ability to shoot
accurately.

His conscience was bothering him. He
felt deep down in his heart that war and
fighting were all wrong. The more he
studied the Bible the more he was convinced of it. At last he went up to his
captain and told him: "Captain, sir, I'm
a tellin' you, and I hain't a foolin' you,
I have done obeyed every order right smart

and I am a-goin' to.   If you order me overseas, I'm a-goin'.   If you put a rifle-gun in
my hands and tell me to kill Germans, I'm
a-goin' to kill them, but I'm a warnin' you,
Captain Danforth, that if you force me to
kill any of my fellow men, I'm a-goin' to
hold you responsible for their lives before
God in Heaven on Judgment Day."   Here
was surely the strangest conscientious objector that ever reported to an American
military camp.   He was a good soldier and
had obeyed all orders and meant to obey
them.   He would fight and kill if ordered
to, but he would hold his captain responsible in the next world.   Fortunately, the
captain was a soldier and a philosopher—
he passed the buck to the major.

By an extraordinary coincidence it happened that Major Buxton had taken part
in Theodore Roosevelt's preparedness campaign before America came in, and in his
addresses through the country had often
been heckled and challenged by ministers
and other religious people who quoted the
Bible to prove that war was wrong.   In
self-defense he, too, had been forced to
study the Bible and had selected and

memorized many passages which seemed to prove that war was not always wrong, and that under certain circumstances it was right for a man to fight for his country. He was just the right sort of man to handle a conscientious objector. Buxton was a very fine soldier, a great American, and a humanitarian who was always interested in hearing and understanding the other fellow's viewpoint. When the captain told him of the mountaineer's scruples, he immediately inquired, "Is he afraid?"

To which Danforth answered, "No, but he has religion, and he has it bad."

The major then told the captain to bring the private to his hut to talk things over.

The story of this extraordinary interview in the major's hut that night in Camp Gordon—and it has been told in detail by the three of them—is one of the most human and beautiful episodes in the military history of this country. It reflects much credit upon the three men concerned, and should win them a very high place in the hearts of their fellow countrymen.

There were no pictures on the walls of the little hut, no carpets on the floor, and very little furniture. A drop light hung down from the whitewashed ceiling. There was an iron military bed along the wall, a small table and chair, a battered military trunk in one corner, and military accouterments hanging all over the place. It was a typical military hut, small, bare, and clean. The major sat on the bed, the captain on the chair, and the private sprawled on the floor. They met, not as two officers and a private, but as three decent Americans trying to figure things out.

After telling Private York that he was a big fellow, a good soldier, a dead shot, and that his pioneer ancestors had been fighters, the major asked him why he did not want to fight when his country needed him.

The mountaineer replied, "Because it is written, 'Thou shalt not kill.' "

"The Christ who drove the money changers out of the temple was a fighter," returned Buxton.

The mountaineer looked at the major with those piercing blue eyes, and with a voice as soft and smooth as velvet, returned, "He done preached, 'Blessed are the peacemakers.' "

"He also preached," came back Buxton, " 'Render unto Cæsar the things that are Cæsar's and unto God the things that are God's.' "

The mountaineer was far from convinced. He looked at the major again quietly, and emphasized that, "He done preached, 'Blessed are the meek.' "

The major switched to the Old Testament and quoted Ezekiel:

"When I bring the sword upon a land, if the people of the land take a man of their coasts, and set him for their watchman:

"If when he seeth the sword come upon the land, he blow the trumpet, and warn the people;

"Then whosoever heareth the sound of the trumpet, and taketh not warning; if the sword come, and take him away, his blood shall be upon his own head.

"He heard the sound of the trumpet, and took not warning; his blood shall be upon him. But he that taketh warning shall deliver his soul.

"But if the watchman see the sword come, and blow not the trumpet, and the

12

people be not warned; if the sword come, and take any person from among them, he is taken away in his iniquity; but his blood will I require at the watchman's hand."

Alvin York listened carefully, allowed the major's quotation to turn over in his mind, and then told him that when St. Peter struck off the ear of the high priest Christ restored the ear and told Peter to put up the sword, with the admonition, "They that live by the sword shall die by the sword."

The extraordinary and beautiful scene continued for over half an hour, with each trying to make his point with well-chosen Biblical passages. The mountaineer, returning to his lines after it was over, informed the captain that he "was most awful glad to know that his major, although he was a New Englander, knowed such a mighty lot about the Bible."

The major, too, was tremendously impressed with the intelligent sincerity of the big fellow. The following morning he sent word that he believed him to be sincere, but that Uncle Sam really needed him.

"Take a couple of weeks' leave," he told
the private. "Go back home and think it
over; then if you can come back with a
free conscience, come back, and we will
take you overseas as a doughboy. But if
you cannot come with a free conscience,
let me know and I will let you out."

The mountaineer wrote in his diary:

> O Master, let me walk with Thee
> In lowly paths of service free;
> Tell me thy secret, help me bear
> The strain of toil, the fret of care.

And that night, in his own words, he "lit
out for the little old log cabin in the valley
and them thar hound dogs of mine, and the
life where I belong."

## Chapter XVII

## "The Sword of the Lord and of Gideon"

THE following day, back home, he slipped into his overalls, shouldered his muzzle-loader, whistled to his hound dogs, and went hunting over the hills. He never fired a shot. He was too worried. His country needed him, and he loved his country. But he was a deeply religious man and was firmly convinced that it was wrong to fight and kill. He could not get past the Lord's command, "Thou shalt not kill." Day after day the struggle within him increased. The blood of his ancestors seemed to call upon him to fight, but the Bible was "agin" it.

He discussed the problem with his family, with his friend, Pastor Pile, and had many a heart-to-heart chat with Gracie. They could not help him. They were simple mountain people and knew little of psychology and even less of the scientific theory

For two days and a night, Alvin York knelt on the mountain side

of the attraction of two opposites. Alvin, too, was untrained in abstract reasoning. He was much more a man of action than a thinker. He turned the problem over and over in his mind. He tried to reconcile the call of his country with the written word of his God. He could not. He had no first-class teacher to confide in, no psychologist to straighten him out. His friends could not help him. It was his problem and his alone. He was "worried a plenty."

Day after day, like a prophet of old, wrestling with his doubts and fears, he tramped the blue mountains of Tennessee. At nighttime, he sat out on a log and earnestly and sincerely tried to figure it out. He got nowhere.

Two days before his leave expired, he did something which, more than anything else, reveals his deeply religious character; something which in this skeptical age should be held up to every man, woman, and child in America as a rock of Gibraltar of faith. Unable to solve the problem himself and unable to receive the help he needed from his friends and loved ones, he put the problem up to his God. For two days and a night, he knelt on the mountain side, alone with his Maker and the primal nakedness of his own soul, and prayed for guidance. The members of his family, Gracie, and a number of mountaineers saw him keep this lonely vigil, and still talk with wonder of it. He prayed and prayed through the long day and the dark night and the day which followed.

At the end of nearly thirty-six hours, something happened to him. He got up off his knees, and he felt, as he explained it later, "like the waters of the lake when the Master said, 'Peace, be still.'" With a gleam in his eyes and buoyancy in his walk, he returned to the little log cabin. His mother saw him coming, and with the intuitive understanding of a mother, cried out, "You're a-goin!"

He looked at her, smiled, and with a faith that was never afterwards to be shaken, said, "I'm a-goin' to war with 'the sword of the Lord and of Gideon.'" When she told him she was "afeared," he took her in his arms and smilingly told her that he was "a-goin' and that he was a-comin' back right smart."

"How do you know that?" she asked. "How can you possibly know it? How can anybody know it?"

There and then he made his declaration: "Because I have received my assurance— I have received it from God himself—that it's right for me to go to war, and that as long as I believe in Him, not one hair of my head will be harmed."

Armed with this faith he was invulnerable.

Let the scoffer laugh and the cynic sneer at him for his simple mountain faith. It worked. He went overseas, and in one of the greatest individual fights in the history of modern or legendary warfare, he whipped single-handed an entire machine-gun battalion. Of all the millions of brave men who fought over there, he was picked out by Marshal Foch himself as the outstanding hero. After it was all over, he returned without one single hair of his head being harmed. His faith worked. It was the faith which "moveth mountains."

Armed with the "sword of the Lord and of Gideon," with the purest Anglo-Saxon blood in the world flowing in his veins, speaking the Old English of Chaucer and Shakespeare, the greatest shot and the mightiest hunter in the mountains went forth to battle, a private in the 328th Battalion of the 82d Division.

## Chapter XVIII

# In the Front Line

IN May, 1918, unknown and unsung, one of the millions of doughboys overseas, Alvin C. York arrived in France. He was bigger than the majority of them, a much better shot, and one of the most spiritual men over there. Otherwise there was nothing to distinguish him from his buddies. His routine and training were exactly the same as theirs. He turned in his American rifle for a British one; slipped on his mask and walked through the gas chambers; indulged in bayonet practice; and, above all, hiked. Like most of the doughboys, he learned quickly that going overseas does not mean rushing straight into the trenches. His division was green and had to be seasoned and toughened by intensive training and gradually worked up to the front line, where in quiet sectors it would receive its baptism of fire.

He stood at attention beside thousands of

other doughboys while Field Marshal Douglas Haig, the British commander in chief, and General Pershing inspected and reviewed the Eighty-second Division.

Often he entrained in those French box cars marked, "Forty men or eight horses." He tells the story of a stupid corporal who was ordered to load one of the cars. After being away for several hours, the corporal returned to the sergeant, saluted, and reported, "I got the forty men in all right, but I hope to tell you, sergeant, if you insist on putting the horses in, too, you will trample them all to death."

From Le Havre to Eu, from Eu to Floraville, from Floraville to Mons Babert, from Mons Babert to Fressenneville, from Fressenneville to Toul, from Toul to Lucey, from Lucey to Rambucourt, he moved with his division up to the front lines. He hiked most of the way—"travelin' a-foot-back," as he called it in his mountain dialect. To a hunter accustomed to roaming the hills of Tennessee, these route marches of fifteen or twenty kilometers were easy, but the city boys were usually tired at the end of the day and reached their destination with

two shoes full of blisters. They grinned
and seldom complained. As they tramped
along the highways and the byways, they
sang, "The Yanks Are Coming," "Dixie,"
and other stirring soldier songs to entertain
the French girls who often lined their route
or leaned out of windows to cheer them on.
Many times, his buddies at night slipped
into the villages, where they drank enormous quantities of red wine and cognac and
painted the *estaminets* vermilion. They
were full of fight and fitter than they had
ever been.

On one occasion, after a few drinks,
some of the Polish boys in the company
stated that the Irishmen could not fight.
That started things. They began with
belts and fists and ended with bottles and
bayonet bosses. Both sides claimed the
victory. According to Alvin, who was
merely an onlooker, "They mussed each
other up right smart."

He never smoked, drank, or bothered
much about the *estaminets* and villages,
but having been through it all on the Tennessee-Kentucky line, he sympathized and
carefully refrained from criticizing. He

was beginning to understand and to love these foreign-born boys in his outfit, and they in turn were growing to admire the big, quiet mountaineer.

Through deserted trenches, over broken wire entanglements, with the shells flashing and roaring in the distance and occasional stray bullets droning like bees past their ears, they moved into the Montsec Sector, and at Rambucourt took over the front lines from the 26th Division.

They were in the trenches at last and were anxious to get at the Germans; and only with difficulty were the officers able to restrain them from going over the top and rushing across No Man's Land—to certain death.

The front-line trenches in this sector were deep and dirty ditches about ten feet deep, wriggling snakelike across the countryside. Alvin took his turn on sentry duty, and often crouching on the parapet while his buddies slept in the trenches below, saw the dawn come up and silhouette the enemy wire entanglements against the morning sky. His first inclination, when he heard a bullet whiz past, was to duck. However,

American graves near the scene of York's fight

he quickly got over that.  "You never hear the one that gets you," he commented grimly.  He learned to judge the size of the shells and to tell by the noise where they were going to burst within a few yards. Quickly he accustomed himself to the star shells and the Verey lights which hissed up from the German lines, exploded and hung like arc lamps over No Man's Land, turning the night into day.  The moment he heard their peculiar sound he ducked for cover.  When out on No Man's Land patroling where there was no cover, he froze immediately in his stride, standing motionless until the light went out again.

It was a hair-raising experience at first. He could see the German trenches plainly through the bright light.  He could see their loopholes and the gleam of the bayonets above the parapet.  It seemed incredible that the enemy could not see him. The first two or three times he held his breath and waited for the staccato bark of a rifle, or the rat-tat-tat of a machine-gun burst.  It never came.  By standing motionless he blended into the background, and the Germans could not see him.

Occasionally he was detailed to "listening post" at night.  He slipped silently over the top, wriggled through the barbed wire, crawled into a shell crater far out on No Man's Land and listened to what was going on all around him and in the German trenches ahead.  This was nerve-racking work at first, but the hunter who had often lain for hours waiting for foxes, or worked through the forest to get a close shot at a turkey gobbler or a deer, soon adapted himself to it.  His deadly skill with a rifle and pistol was, of course, known to his officers, and it was inevitable that he should be given a chance to exploit it.

After a few days in the front line, he was put in charge of an automatic rifle squad which patroled No Man's Land after dark. Armed with French "shoshos," they scouted quietly up and down between the two lines. These French automatic rifles were not very reliable.  They made a great racket, but seldom hit anything.  Alvin more than once had good cause to regret the absence of his old muzzle-loader.  He knew, of course, that for rapidity of fire and accuracy over long ranges it could not compare with the army rifles.  Nevertheless, his fingers occasionally twitched to caress its long, smooth barrel.

Being unusually observant, he learned quickly to protect himself against the deadly gas.  His keen ear noted instantly the soft explosion of the shells, and he seldom had to be told to put on his mask.  Occasionally, if the wind was blowing in the direction of the American trenches, the Germans sent the gas over in the form of clouds, or rather of a fog bank.  Sometimes it lingered in the bottom of trenches and dugouts for several hours.  One had always to be on the lookout for it.  It smelled very much like the odor of rotten pears.

It was summer time in the trenches, and gas masks and shrapnel helmets were hot and heavy.  The doughboys preferred to do without them, but after a few had complained of dizzy headaches and started vomiting and clutching at their burning throats and others had fallen in their tracks under a shower of shrapnel fragments, the boys learned what was good for them and wore their masks and helmets when ordered. The big mountaineer observed all this, and while he had no fear and never went out of his way to protect himself, on the other hand, he was too sensible to take unnecessary chances when the army provided such protection as gas masks and shrapnel helmets. Once or twice some shrapnel fragments or spent bullets whanged against his helmet. He merely grinned and carried on.

In common with all soldiers, he learned quickly that the spade is almost as valuable a part of the soldier's equipment as the rifle and bayonet. He was as good as the best of them when it came to filling sandbags, digging ditches, making roads, and doing the other chores of the soldier on active service. Of course, it would be unfair to the others to say that he was a braver fighter or a harder worker than his buddies. He would be the last one to claim this. He was just one of them, a good, brave, hard-working doughboy.

Throughout it all his faith never wavered. It sustained him in the dugouts and trenches and out in No Man's Land. It was his "pillar of cloud by day" and "pillar of fire by night." He prayed regularly and earnestly and felt his God ever at his side watching over him—a reality. The first night in the trenches he wrote in his diary what has since been described as the most spiritual utterance of the World War:

Montsec Sector, France

There is no use of worrying a Bout Shells for you cant keep them from bursting in your trench nor you cant Stop the rain or prevent a light from going up jes' as you are halfway over the parapet—so what is the use of worrying if you cant alter things just ask God to help you and accept them and make the best of them by the help of God.

Captain Danforth was watching him carefully and had him marked out for early promotion. The conscientious objector was making good over there in France.

## Chapter XIX

## Buddies

WAR brings men together, strips the masks off, and reveals them in all their strength and weakness. A week in the trenches teaches you more about your fellow men than you would normally learn in a lifetime.

Drilling, parading, and route marching at home in Camp Gordon, packed together like sardines in a transport going overseas, eating, sleeping, and hiking beyond the lines in France, marching shoulder to shoulder and blade to blade to the lilt of the rollicking soldiers' songs, in the lousy dugouts and dirty trenches, with death always in the air, living intimately with each other week after week and month after month, the doughboys got to know and understand each other.

Alvin's eyes were opened. His buddies were different from his old friends in the mountains, but in their own way were just

(180)

as fine.  There was something about them
that appealed to him.  Their bravery, their
loyal comradeship, their radiant optimism
in the face of hardship and death quickly
endeared them to him.

Captain C. E. B. Danforth, Jr., company
commander, was a tall, willowy Southerner,
from Augusta, Georgia.  The finest blood
in the South flowed in his veins.  He was a
gallant American gentleman, handsome,
fearless, and understanding.  Along with
his battalion commander, Major Buxton,
he was the first to understand and appreciate for their full worth the sterling qualities of the big mountaineer.  The captain
shared in common with his men all the
hardships and terrors of trench warfare.
He asked them to endure nothing he was
not willing to endure himself.  He was
always first over the top.

The platoon sergeant, Harry Parsons, of
Brooklyn, New York, was a vaudeville
actor who had left the theater for the
trenches.  He was a black-haired, blue-
eyed, strapping big fellow, and the right
sort of man to handle the wild outfit under
him.  He was equally good with tongue or

fists, and was a rough, mean fellow to cross the wrong way. He never looked for trouble, but if he saw it coming, he was always able to handle it. He was a fine soldier and a good singer; and when feet were tired and shoulders drooping after a long day's march, his beautiful voice often lilted out in a popular song which lifted the drooping spirits of his men and spurred them on. Sergeant Parsons was responsible for the order which sent the seventeen doughboys through the Argonne forest after the machine guns. Something happened to Parsons that morning. He was never again the same happy-go-lucky, laughing, singing, good-natured doughboy. After the Armistice he returned to the vaudeville stage, where he found to his dismay he was no longer able to make his audience laugh. He left his laugh in the Argonne forest that October morning.

Corporal, later Acting Sergeant, Bernard Early, who led the detail against the machine guns, was a naturalized Irishman from New Haven, Connecticut. According to his registration card in the archives of the War Department in Washington, he

had had been a bartender before the war.
He looked and acted the part to perfection.
"Bernie" had all of the reckless daring and
winning charm of the Irish. He loved
nothing better than to drink and curse and
fight. He was a past master at each.
Leave breaking with him was a science.
He went A. W. O. L. again and again.
His officers frequently "busted" him, only
to reinstate him a few days later. Bernard
Early was a good soldier, a born scrapper,
and a leader of men.

His buddy was Corporal William Cutting,
an iceman from Boston. Unknown to his
comrades, he was in the army under an
assumed name. His real name was Meri-
thew. He, too, could put his liquor away,
and, like Early, knew how to curse and
scrap. He was as hard as nails and declared
openly that if bombs were thrown at him,
he would eat them for breakfast. Although
pretty nearly shot to pieces in the fight
with the machine guns, he walked out with
the slightly wounded cases. When Parsons
greeted him later behind the American
lines, he was weak from loss of blood and
vomiting with pain, but he grinned, waved

a captured German Luiger pistol, and exclaimed, "I got what I wanted!" When Early and Cutting became fighting mad, either in the camp or in the front-line trenches, something was sure to happen, and somebody was bound to get hurt. They caused their officers a great deal of trouble. They caused the Germans much more.

Corporal Murray Savage was a farmer from "up state" in New York; a quiet, unobstrusive chap, and one of the very best soldiers in the company. He fell that morning in the Argonne with over two hundred bullets in his body. When they tried to pick him up after the battle, his clothes came off him in little pieces. He had been Alvin York's buddy.

Among the privates was Michael Saccina, a little Italian. After the machine-gun fight he compared the captured German major's whistle to the little whistle on a peanut stand on the east side of New York City. It is not hard to picture him.

Private Theodore Sok was a quiet, phlegmatic doughboy with a smoldering volcano somewhere in his make-up. When it broke out, which was seldom, it was just too bad for those around. The Germans at Saint-Mihiel and in the Argonne forest would testify to this. He was always referred to as "Sok," or "Sock." A number of the boys in his company, including Alvin York, thought that this really was his nickname.

Joe Konotski, Walter Swanson, Muzzi, Beardsley, and Johnson were among the others who made up that hard-boiled, hard-fighting, and recklessly brave company of American doughboys.

They combined in their lives and records over there the patriotism, the happy-go-lucky spirit, courage, steadfastness, and tragedy of the soldier engaged in arms. They endured all uncomplainingly.

In the Saint-Mihiel drive one of the privates disappeared during the thick of the fighting. Shortly afterwards a non-commissioned officer caught him leading a goat across the battle field. On being asked where on earth he was going with the goat, he grinned and replied, "Sergeant, I am just going back to put a little cream in my coffee."

When they were first issued safety razors in America, two of the foreign-born boys indulged in the following conversation:

FIRST PRIVATE: Anything the government gives you for nothing is no good. This fool razor won't cut.

SECOND PRIVATE: I never did like the Democrats, and now that they are in power they give us blunt razors. Can you beat it?

They both threw their razors on the ground. They knew so little about safety razors that they were actually trying to shave themselves without having first removed the wax paper from the blades!

After Captain Danforth had voluntarily led the remnants of his company to its objective immediately following Alvin York's victorious attack upon the machine guns, he was returning to headquarters, accompanied by his striker, who was of Austrian birth and had been a tailor's assistant before the war. Suddenly the captain saw thirty or forty Germans waving from a near-by hillside. Their attitude appeared friendly enough, but he was taking no chances. He waited until they threw down their weapons, held up their hands, surrendered, and came out in the open. Then, with the help of the Austrian, he made them prisoners and marched them back to headquarters. These were the survivors of the machine-gun battalion which the mountaineer had shot up a few hours before. Captain Danforth gallantly asserts that inasmuch as York had smashed up their battalion, thus isolating and forcing them to surrender, he should also be credited with their capture.

The striker was a little fellow who had probably never fired a gun in his life. He was kept back at headquarters, tailoring and doing odd jobs. However, he must have been a little Napoleon in disguise. The moment he realized that the Germans were helpless he seemed to grow several inches in stature. He raised his head like a bantam fighting cock about to crow. Able to speak German, he ordered two of the prisoners to present him with their revolvers. Then he called out a few orders in German and pointed the revolver threateningly at the prisoners, until a box of cigars was produced. More orders and more

threatening looks and a bottle of wine was
presented.   With a pistol in each hand, a
big, fat cigar stuck in his mouth, a box of
them under one arm, and a bottle of wine
under the other, he turned to the captain
and assured him that he was awaiting his
orders.

These soldiers in Alvin York's company
were real doughboys and among the most
human men who ever donned American
uniforms.

The big mountaineer learned to love them
with a great love.   Again and again he
mentions them in his diary.   On one occasion when one of them was killed he lay
out beside his dead body all night, praying
for him.   After he had whipped and im-
prisoned the machine gunners in the
Argonne, he ordered the prisoners to carry
out the American wounded.   They were
his buddies, and he was not going to leave
them out there in the heart of the forest to
die.   His tribute to his buddies, as printed
in the foreword of his biography is one of
the most beautiful tributes ever paid by a
distinguished American soldier to his companions in the firing line:

TO
OUR OWN
LEAGUE OF NATIONS

The American-born boys and the Greeks, Irish,
Poles, Jews, and Italians who were in my platoon
in the World War.  A heap of them couldn't speak
or write the American language until they larned
it in the army.  Over here in the training camps
and behind the lines in France a right-smart lot of
them boozed, gambled, cussed and went A. W. O. L.
But once they got into it Over There they kept on
agoing.  They were only tol'able shots and burned
up a most awful lot of ammunition.  But jest the
same they always kept on a-going.  Most of them
died like men, with their rifles and bayonets in their
hands and their faces to the enemy.  I'm a thinkin'
they were real heroes.  Any way they were my
buddies.  I jes' learned to love them.*

---

\* *Sergeant York—His Own Life Story and War Diary.*  Edited
by Tom Skeyhill.  Published by Doubleday, Doran & Company.

## CHAPTER XX

# The Battle of the Argonne

IN September, the 82d Division participated in the Saint-Mihiel drive, the first major offensive of the United States army. The Germans refused to stand and match either bullets or bayonets with the doughboys. They hurriedly retreated.

Alvin and his buddies were right in the thick of it. The big fellow distinguished himself and was promoted to corporal.

The morale of the division could not possibly have been better. The doughboys had been under fire for several weeks now, were accustomed to trench warfare and open fighting, and had been in the front waves of a successful offensive.

Their faith in their great leader, General Pershing, was absolute. His plan of attack at Saint-Mihiel was perfect. Everything had worked with the cold accuracy of science and the deadly precision of clockwork. The German positions were taken with a minimum of casualties on the American side.

In the middle of September, in the best of spirits, a little flushed with the sweet wine of victory, laughing and singing as they marched, or rode in the big French busses, they moved north again, and in late September encamped on the outskirts of the Argonne forest. The "big push" was on. The American army was smashing its way through the forest in an attempt to land a knock-out punch on the reeling but desperate German army. The 82d Division was held in reserve on the fringe of the forest for several days.

To Alvin, the forest was an abomination of desolation, and the battle was Armageddon. In his own expressive dialect he wrote that "the place was mussed up right smart." It looked as if a tornado had swept through, smashing and leveling the trees, ripping holes in the ground, and tossing human bodies on all sides until the forest looked more like a shambles than anything else.

Night and day, the low thunder of the big guns rolled in from the front lines, shaking the earth and causing occasional rain showers, but the doughboys were used to it now; they did not mind it, nor lose any sleep because of it. Airplanes circled and droned overhead, and the men witnessed many thrilling air duels and saw a number of planes go down in flames. After seeing such a tragedy, one of the boys remarked that he "might be killed by an airplane—he might—but it would have to land on him."

The tanks, snorting and chugging up toward the front, looked for all the world like ponderous, slow-moving, heavily armored prehistoric monsters. Ambulances and supply wagons passed in endless procession. Slightly wounded soldiers, with muddy uniforms, unshaven chins, and feverish-looking eyes, staggered past on their way to the dressing stations. The woods were full of corpses, Germans and Americans. There had been no time to bury them. Broken and snarled wire entanglements, deserted trenches half full of stagnant water, innumerable shell craters, wrecked guns and abandoned tanks all bore mute witness to the terrific struggle which had raged through this part of the forest only a few days before.

Alvin and his buddies were impatient to be in the thick of the battle. They "strained like greyhounds on the leash." Nevertheless, the higher commands continued to hold them in reserve.

Corporal York often slipped into the woods, alone, at night and pondered over the eternal mystery of things. Scarcely more than a year ago, he had been in other woods, in another land, hunting coon, possum, squirrel, and fox. Now he was hunting his fellow men.

He puzzled his mind, trying to recall whether he had ever heard or seen anything as terrible as this battle of the Argonne. He knew he never had. He recalled all the cruel things he had ever seen animals do—dogs, wild cats, coons, and bears. He knew that in their cruelest moments he had never seen them do anything as terrible as his fellow beings were doing here in the Argonne. It came home to him that man in war is more cruel and destroys more deliberately and on a bigger scale than any other living thing in the world.   He wondered why.   He loved his fellow men with a great love.   He wanted to understand them, but all of this hating and killing and destroying was very hard to understand.    Surely,  it must be Armageddon.

Often when he was tired and wet, when the blackness of the forest was torn by the flashes and screams of shells and the machine guns in the front line profaned the silence with their never-ceasing staccato, he thought of home and loved ones.   On such occasions the little log cabin in the valley seemed far away.

On the night of October 7, 1918, the long and eagerly awaited order came for the Eighty-second to move up and take over a sector of the front line.   Shortly after midnight they started.

Corporal York wrote in his diary that they tripped over dead men and dead horses, were wet through, dirty and tired, and often had to leave the road and crouch in the ditches as the artillery thundered past.   A big German shell burst right in the midst of some of his buddies, and he wrote: "Oh, my agony, no tongue can tell."

Crossing over a little bridge, another big shell screamed through the night, exploded with a terrific detonation and mangled and wiped out a couple of squads. For a time his company was lost in the unfathomable darkness of the forest.

But Captain Danforth never gave up and kept leading them toward where he believed the trenches to be. Shortly before daylight the little company, wet to the skin and very nearly exhausted, climbed a small hill marked 223 on the war maps and took over a sector of the front line. The exact position was almost nine miles in front of Varennes, immediately ahead of Chatel Chehery and a little to the rear and left of the village of Carnay. At dawn the attack was to begin, and the big red-headed mountaineer from the Valley of the Three Forks of the Wolf was to write a thrilling and almost unbelievable page in the military history of the United States Army.

## CHAPTER XXI

## The Official Story

CORPORAL YORK'S capture of the German machine-gun battalion was so incredible that at first even the Army officers refused to believe it. They held investigation after investigation until they were completely convinced. From that day to this, his stanchest supporters and champions have been Captain Danforth, his company commander, Major Buxton, his original battalion commander, and the high-ranking officers of the American army, from Brigadier General Lindsay through Generals Leggett and Summerall right up to General Pershing himself.

When Alvin York invited me to write his official biography and I began to sink a shaft into the story, I frankly admit I was skeptical. I could not get used to the idea that one American doughboy had whipped a German machine-gun battalion. I knew that my doubts would be shared by millions of other people.  I therefore made up my mind to spend almost a year of my life carefully checking the records, tracking down, interviewing, and obtaining affidavits from the survivors.  Through the courtesy of the officers of the War Department, I was given access to the official archives. I examined and copied every single official paper.  There were hundreds of them. I cannot imagine a military deed that has been submitted to a closer scrutiny and that has been so carefully investigated over and over again as Alvin York's feat in the Argonne that morning.  The records cannot lie.  They proved beyond any possible shadow of a doubt that the big fellow did everything that has ever been claimed he did, and more.

I visited Major Buxton, the original commander of Alvin's battalion, and the official historian of the division.  He had several boxes of records, all of which he placed at my disposal.  In Augusta, Georgia, I located the company commander, Captain Danforth, discussed the fight with him, examined his records, obtained his affidavit, and a few days later accompanied him into the mountains to visit and shoot with the sergeant. I spent several days with the platoon sergeant, Harry Parsons, who issued the order to attack the machine guns; and together we visited Sergeant Bernard Early, in New Haven, Connecticut. I obtained the affidavits of these two gallant soldiers, and through the War Department and the divisional historian, I collected the affidavits of Privates Muzzi, Beardsley, Konotski, Sok, Saccina, Donohue, and Wills. I have never been able to locate or find any statement ever made by Private Thomas C. Johnson. If this book ever comes to his notice or that of any of his friends, I wish he would communicate with me through the publishers.

I also have in my possession a copy of Alvin York's affidavit, taken shortly after the fight. Of course, in the years I have known him intimately, I have heard from his own lips and have had taken down in shorthand every detail as far as he remembers it of what happened in the forest that morning. Thus, of the eleven survivors, I have collected the affidavits of nine, as well as those of the platoon sergeant, company commander, and official historian. I have also in my possession the affidavit of Lieutenant Joseph A. Woods, the intelligence officer who counted the prisoners when York brought them in.

Here is Captain Danforth's own story of what happened that historic morning:

At 6 A. M. on the morning of October 8, 1918, the 2d Battalion, 328th Infantry, attacked from Hill 223, in the direction ten degrees north of west, with its objective, the Decauville Railroad, about three kilometers away. The battalion had moved into the Argonne sector with other units of the 82d Division on the night of October 6 and 7. All the day of October 7 we lay along the main army road, running from Varennes to Fleville, and watched the attack of the 1st Battalion, which in the early afternoon gained the height of Hill 223.

About 2 A. M., October 8, the regimental commander sent for the company commanders of the 2d Battalion and issued instructions for the attack of the Battalion to be made from Hill 223 at 6 A. M. I was in command of Company G of this battalion and immediately upon receiving these instructions began moving my company across the Aire River to the designated jump-off line on Hill 223.

I reached this hill at 5.50 A. M. and deployed my company for assault in two waves, two platoons in the front wave and two platoons in the supporting wave. The left support platoon was commanded by Sergeant Harry M. Parsons, one of his corporals being Alvin C. York.

At zero hour we began the advance, moving down the slope of Hill 223 and across the five-hundred-yard open valley toward a steep wooded hill to our immediate front. On our right was E Company, 328th Infantry, on our left Unit 5 of the 28th Division, though throughout the entire day we had no contact whatsoever with these troops on our left.

Upon reaching about the center of this valley we were stopped by a withering fire of machine guns from the front, from the unscalable heights of the Champrocher Ridge on our right and from a heavily wooded hill on our left. From this point the advance was very slow, the men moving by rushes from shell hole to shell hole a few feet at a time. At some time during the morning the fire from the left flank slackened and we were enabled to gain the hill to our immediate front, capturing a great many machine guns and driving the enemy to the west. During the progress of the fighting across this valley, I was with the assault waves and gave no orders for the employment of the support platoons, which had been ordered to follow at three hundred yards.

About noon I left the assault wave and with one runner returned to bring up my support platoons, running into a group of forty-four Germans in the edge of the woods just outside our left flank, which group surrendered to my runner and me without

firing a shot at us.   I sent these prisoners to the
rear, located my support platoons, returned with
them to the front lines, and at 4 P. M. continued the
advance to the corps objective with the other com-
panies of the 2d Battalion.   This objective—the
Decauville Railroad—we took about 5 P. M.   With
the handful of men that were left we organized a
position and held it throughout the night of October
8 and 9.

On the morning of October 9 at about ten o'clock
Corporal York with seven men reported to me on
the railroad.   Corporal York, when questioned
about his whereabouts and activities during the
previous day's fighting, said that he had been sent
with a detachment to silence some machine-gun
nests on the left of the valley, that this detachment
had become heavily engaged, losing half its strength,
and that he had captured about one hundred and
fifty prisoners.   He stated that all noncommissioned officers of the detachment had been killed
or wounded, that he had taken command and had
shot a number of Germans during the engagement
and that he had carried his prisoners from headquarters, finally delivering them to the military
police many miles to the rear.   His statement to
me on the morning of October 9 was the first time
that I knew anything of his fight on our left flank and
offered the best explanation of why the fire from
that point had slackened on the morning of the 8th.

After coming out of the lines I fully investigated
this detachment's fight and recommended Corporal

York for the Distinguished Service Cross, and later, after a more careful study, for the Congressional Medal of Honor.

Sergeant Harry Parsons, who issued the order to attack the machine guns, gives us a thrilling picture of the initial stages of the fight in this illuminating affidavit:

I was the platoon sergeant of the 1st Platoon, G Company, 2d Battalion, 328th Infantry, 82d Division; we had no commissioned officer, and I was in charge of the platoon. The platoon was made up of Greeks, Slavs, Swedes, Jews, Irish, Germans, and Italians, all American citizens, of course. There were also a number of farmers and a few mountaineers, one of whom was Alvin C. York. On the morning of October 8, 1918, we marched through the town of Chatel Chehery, and up on to Hill 223, where we waited for the zero hour. Without artillery support we went over the top at about daylight. Our platoon was upon the extreme left flank of the division and was in the second wave, about one hundred yards in the rear of the first. The Germans quickly opened on us with machine guns, securely entrenched in the ridges and brush on our front and left flank. Our first line was mowed down; Lieutenant Stewart was killed and the survivors were forced to dig in. The machine-gun fire was something terrible. If the advance was to be continued, somehow or other the machine guns would have to be put out; and I knew the advance had to be continued at all costs. Our company commander, Captain Danforth, was over on the right, on the other side of the hill, fighting against desperate odds. I had no opportunity of getting in touch with him and he had no chance whatever of getting over to us. But I figured at all cost the machine guns had to be silenced. It was an awful responsibility for a noncommissioned officer to order his men to go to what looked to be certain death. But I figured it had to be done. I figured they had a slight chance of getting the machine guns. So I made the decision—and I now know that it was the wisest decision I ever made. I ordered the left half of my platoon, what remained of four squads, to deploy through the heavy brush on the left and work their way over the ridges to where the German machine guns were firing—and then attack the machine guns and put them out of commission. Sergeant Early was in charge of the four sections, and Corporal York, Corporal Cutting, and Corporal Savage were in charge of the squads. The thirteen private soldiers were privates Dymowski, Wiley, Waring, Swanson, Muzzi, Beardsley, Konotski, Sok, Johnson, Saccina, Donohue, and Wills. Led by Sergeant Early, as ordered, the men immediately advanced through the brush on our left flank and disappeared. A few minutes later we heard heavy firing from the direction which they had taken; and shortly after the German machine-gun fire ceased. It was after this that Corporal York and seven privates returned with 132 German prisoners. Corporal York marched in front of the prisoners and was in absolute command. Unquestionably, the silencing of these machine guns played a tremendous part in our success in finally reaching our objective.

Sergeant Bernard Early, who was in charge of the detail that started out to silence the machine guns, is equally enlightening in his affidavit:

As senior noncommissioned officer in charge of the left half of 1st Platoon, G Company, 2d Battalion, 328th Infantry, 82d Division, on the morning of October 8, 1918, I led what remained of our squads, totaling seventeen men, from the valley under Hill 223 in the Argonne forest around our left flank in an attempt to silence German machine guns which were holding up my battalion's advance to the Decauville Railroad which was our objective.

My command was on the extreme left of our division. I led my men through the thick undergrowth about half a mile toward where we figured the German machine guns were. Then I decided to swing in behind and attack them from the rear. On account of the nature of the country, the Germans were unable to see us, just as we were unable to see them. So far we had no casualties. When we were well behind the German lines, we surprised a German stretcher bearer, who immediately ran and we trailed him through the undergrowth deeper in behind the German lines.

We jumped a little stream and suddenly unexpectedly discovered the headquarters of a German machine-gun regiment. There must have been at least one hundred Germans, including three officers and several noncommissioned officers. There were also runners, orderlies, and others. They were having breakfast and we completely surprised them. We fired several shots to intimidate them and rushed them with fixed bayonets. I was out in front leading them and, seeing the Germans throwing up their hands, I ordered my men to cease fire and to cover and close in on them. I then ordered my men to line them up preparatory to marching them back to our P. C.

In the act of turning around issuing this order, a burst of machine-gun bullets struck me. I fell with one bullet through my arm and five through the lower part of my body. I called on Corporal Cutting to take command and get the prisoners out and if possible later on come back and get me.

A little later Corporal Cutting was wounded and Corporal York took command.

I was carried back with the German prisoners to our first-aid station. There I was operated on and some of the bullets were taken out and I was sent to the hospital.

Here is the affidavit of the intelligence officer who counted the prisoners:

On the morning of October 8, 1918, I was battalion adjutant, 328th Infantry. The battalion P. C. had been moved forward from Hill 223 to a hillside across the valley and just west of Hill 223, the jumping-off place.   We heard some heavy and almost continuous firing on the other side of our hill and in the direction taken by Sergeant Early, Corporal York, and their detachment.   Some time later I personally saw Corporal York and seven privates returning from the hillside on which our P. C. was located. They had 132 prisoners with them, including three German officers, one a battalion commander.   I personally counted the prisoners when Corporal York reported the detachment and prisoners.   Corporal York was in entire charge of this party and was marching at the head of the column with the German officers.   The seven men with Corporal York were scattered along the flanks and rear of the column. Sergeant Early and Corporal Cutting, both severely wounded, were being assisted in the rear of the column.

Here is another check of Lieutenant Woods:

I certify that I personally counted the prisoners reported to the P. C. of the 2nd Battalion, 328th Infantry, by Corporal Alvin C. York, Company G, 328th Infantry, on October 8, 1918, and found them to be 132 in number.

Here is another interesting document. It is the affidavit of Captain Bertrand Cox, who was the first officer to pass over the battle field after the fight:

On the morning of October 8th, I commanded a support platoon of F Company, 2nd Battalion of 328th Infantry.  Shortly after Corporal York and his detachment of seven men succeeded in capturing the greater part of a German battalion, I advanced with my platoon and passed the scene of the fight, which took place before this capture was accomplished.  The ground was covered with German equipment and I should estimate that there were between 20 and 25 dead Germans on the scene of the fight.

All of this evidence is sworn to and included in the official records and proves for all time the authenticity of York's extraordinary feat.  No intelligent person can study these documents without admitting that York did it.  Only those who have not examined the records can ever doubt that this great American soldier practically single-handed whipped and captured a German machine-gun battalion.

## CHAPTER XXII

## York's Own Story

HERE is his own story, copied word for word, from the official documents in the archives of the War Department in Washington. It was taken down shortly after the fight and remains today the clearest and most convincing story of the thrilling episode.

It is supplemented by this official explanation:

The records of the 82d Division reveal no more extraordinary act of individual gallantry and achievement than is accredited, after careful investigation, to Sergeant Alvin C. (No. 1,910,426) York, Co. G, 328th Infantry. York is a farmer, 31 years old, whose home is located at Pall Mall, Tenn., in the mountainous and northeastern corner of the state.

On the 8th of October, 1918, York was a corporal in G Company, 328th Infantry. This company was the left assault company of the 2d Battalion, which jumped off from the crest of Hill 223 just north of Chatel Chehery and attacked due west, with its objective, the Decauville Railroad, two kilometers due west. The success of this assault had a far-reaching effect in relieving the enemy pressure against American forces in the heart of the Argonne Forest. The local success achieved by this battalion was, in itself, of outstanding proportions. About 300 prisoners were taken and nearly 200 dead Germans left on the ground and material captured, which included four 77's, a trench mortar battery, a complete signal outfit and 123 machine guns. The attack was driven through in spite of resistance of a very savage character and most destructive enemy machine-gun and artillery fire. The battalion suffered enfilade fire from both flanks.

The part which Corporal York individually played in this attack is difficult to estimate fully. Practically unassisted, he captured 132 Germans (three of whom were officers), took about 35 machine guns and killed no less than 25 of the enemy, later found by others on the scene of York's extraordinary exploit. York is well known in his section of Tennessee for his remarkable skill with both rifle and pistol.

The following story has been carefully checked in every possible detail from headquarters of this division and is entirely substantiated.

Although Sergeant York's statement tends to underestimate the desperate odds which he overcame, it has been decided to forward to higher authority the account given in his own words:

\* \* \* \* \*

"Sergeant Harry M. Parsons was in command of a platoon of which my squad was a part. This platoon was the left support platoon of G Company, my squad forming the extreme left flank of the platoon.  The valley was covered by machine-gun fire from the right (pointing at the map), from the front, and from the left front.  Machine guns from the left front were causing a great deal of damage to our troops advancing across the valley.  Sergeant Parsons was ordered to advance with his platoon and cover our left flank.  As the fire was very hot in the valley, we decided to skirt the foot of the hill on our left and thereby gain some protection.  We had advanced a little ways up to about here (pointing at the map) when we were held up, by machine guns from our left front here (pointing at the map) Sergeant Parsons told Sergeant Bernard Early to take two squads and put these machine guns out of business; so my squad being the left squad, was one of those chosen.

"We advanced in single file.  The undergrowth and bushes here were so thick that we could see only a few yards ahead of us, but as we advanced, they became a little thinner.  In order to avoid frontal fire from the machine guns, we turned our course slightly to the left, thereby working around on the right flank of the machine guns and somewhat to their rear, which caused us to miss these forward guns (pointing at the map).  As we gained a point about here (pointing at the map and designating a point somewhat in the rear of the machine guns), we turned sharply to the right oblique and followed a little path which took us directly in rear of the

machine guns.   As we advanced we saw two Boche
with Red Cross bands on their arms.   We called
to them to halt, but they did not stop and we opened
fire on them.   Sergeant Early was leading and I
was third.

"As I said before, we were proceeding in single file.
We immediately dashed down a path, along which
the Boche were running, and crossed this stream
(pointing at map).   The Boche then turned to the
right and ran in the direction from which we had
come.   When we reached the point where they
turned, we stopped for half a second to form a
skirmish line.   I jumped about four paces away from
a sergeant and we told the other men to scatter out
because we thought there was going to be a battle
and we did not want to be too close together.   As
soon as we formed our skirmish line, we burst through
the bushes after the Boche.

"This little stream of which I spoke runs through
a gulch into the valley.   On either side of the stream
there was a little stretch of flat, level ground, about
twenty feet wide, which was covered with extremely
thick bush.   On the east bank of the stream was a
hill having an exceedingly steep slope.   The hill was
somewhat semicircular in shape and afforded excellent protection to anyone behind it.   Along the top
of the hill were the machine guns firing across the
valley at our troops.

"We burst through the undergrowth and were
upon the Germans before we knew it, because the
undergrowth was so thick that we could see only a

few yards ahead of us.   There was a little shack thrown together that seemed to be used as a sort of P. C. by the Germans.   In front of this, in a sort of semicircular mass, sat about seventy-five Boche, and beside a chow can, which was near the P. C., sat the commanding officer.   The Boche seemed to be having some kind of conference.

"When we burst in on the circle, some of the Boche jumped and threw up their hands, shouting 'Kamerad.'   Then the others jumped up, and we began shooting.   About two or three Germans were hit.   None of our men fell.

"Sergeant Early said, 'Don't shoot any more. They are going to give up anyhow,' and for a moment our fire ceased, except that one German continued to fire at me, and I shot him.   In the meantime, the Boche upon the hill with the machine guns swung the left guns to the left oblique and opened fire on us.   I was at this time just a few paces from the mass of Boche who were crowded around the P. C.   At the first burst of fire from the machine guns, all the Boche in this group hit the ground, lying flat on their stomachs.   I, and a few other of our men, hit the ground at the same time.   Those who did not take cover were either killed or wounded by the Boche machine-gun fire, the range being so close that the clothes were literally torn from their bodies.   Sergeant Early and Corporal Cutting were wounded, and Corporal Savage was killed.   In this first fire we had six killed and three wounded.   By this time, those of my men who were left had gotten behind trees, and two men sniped at the Boche. They fired about half a clip each. But there wasn't any tree for me, so I just sat in the mud and used my rifle, shooting at the Boche machine gunners. I am a pretty good shot with the rifle, also with the pistol, having used them practically all my life, and having had a great deal of practice. I shot my rifle until I did not have any more clips convenient and then I used my pistol.

"The Boche machine-gun fire was sweeping over the mass of Germans who were lying flat, and passing a few inches over my head, but I was so close to the mass of Germans who were lying down that the Boche machine gunners could not hit me without hitting their own men. There were about fifty Boche with the machine guns, and they were under the command of a lieutenant. By this time, the remaining Boche guns had turned around and were firing at us, and the lieutenant with eight or ten Germans armed with rifles rushed toward us. One threw a little grenade about the size of a dollar and with a string that you pull like this when you want it to explode, at me, but missed me by a few feet, wounding, however, one of his own men.

"I just let the Boche come down the hill and then poured it into them with my pistol, and I am, as I said before, a pretty good shot with a pistol. I shot the lieutenant, and when he was killed, the machine-gun fire ceased. During the fight I kept hearing a pistol firing from the midst of the Boche who were lying on the ground. This was evidently the commanding officer shooting, as he was the only one in the crowd armed with a pistol, and all of his clips were empty when I examined them later.

"When the machine guns ceased firing, the commanding officer, who spoke English, got off the ground and walked over to me.  He said, 'English?' I said, 'No, not English.'  He said, 'What?'  I said, 'American.'  He said, 'Good Lord!'  Then he said, 'If you won't shoot any more, I will make them give up,' and I said, 'Well, all right, I will treat you like a man,' and he turned around and said something to his men in German, and they all threw off their belts and arms and the machine gunners threw down their arms and came down the hill.

"I called to my men and one of them answered me over here, another from over there, and another here (they were pretty well scattered), and when they all come to me, I found that there were six left besides myself.

"We searched the Boche and told them to line up in a column of twos.  The Boche commanding officer wanted to line up facing north and go down through the valley along the road which runs by the foot of the hill, but I knew if they got me there it would be as good as they wanted on account of the machine guns on the opposite slope, so I said, 'No, I am going this way, which was the way I had come, and which led through the group of machine guns placed here (pointing at the map), which seemed to be outpost guns.  We had missed this machine-gun nest as we advanced, because we had gone farther to the left.

"When we got the Boche lines up in a column of twos, I scattered my men along and at the rear of the column and told them to stay well to the rear and that I would lead the way. So I took the commanding officer and the other two officers and put one in front of me and one on each side of me, and we headed the column. I did that because I knew that if I were caught on the side of the column, the machine gunners would shoot me, but that if I kept in the column, they would have to shoot their officers before they could kill me. In this manner we advanced along a path and into the machine-gun nest which is situated here (pointing at the map).

"The machine-gunners, as I said before, could not kill me without killing their officers, and I was ready for them. One aimed a rifle at me from behind a tree, and, as I pointed my pistol at him, the commanding officer said, 'If you won't shoot any more, I will tell them to surrender.' He did and we added them to our column.

"I then reported with the prisoners to the battalion P. C. They were counted there and there were 132 of them. I was there ordered to deliver the prisoners to brigade headquarters, which I did, and returned to my company the next morning."

Here, then, is the whole truth of the York story, told by himself, by his buddies and officers, and by the official records.

## Chapter XXIII

## Prisoners

THE opening chapter in this story ended with the German major with York's pistol between his eyes, blowing his whistle, and the machine gunners surrendering. The big fellow had "shot up" and whipped the battalion and forced the Germans to "Kamerad," but much remained to be done. He was deep in the forest, far behind the German lines, with over one hundred prisoners on his hands and only a few dough-boys to help get them out. The story of how he accomplished this almost impossible task has already been told in the affidavits, but it is an immortal story and can bear repeating and explaining.

The moment the firing stopped, the Germans in the machine-gun trench threw down their weapons and equipment, and with their hands raised high above their heads, came down the hillside toward him. one of them had a small bomb in his hand,

and thinking that the big mountaineer was
off guard, hurled it at his head.   York
ducked and at the same moment planted
a shot between the thrower's eyes.   He
commanded the major to motion the other
officers to his side, and after he had done
so, using the major as an interpreter,
threatened to shoot them first if there was
another shot fired, or a suspicious movement made.   He called the doughboys to
help him line up the prisoners in column of
twos and march them out.   One of them
furtively exclaimed, "We cannot do it.
There is not enough of us."   York promptly
told him to shut up.   The captured major
inquired, "How many men have you got?"
York turned and answered, "I've got a
plenty.   Keep your hands up."   He lined
up the German prisoners in a column of
twos and placed two doughboys with bayonets and bombs on each side and two in
the rear.   He took the head of the column
himself, with the major in front of him and
a German officer on each side as a shield.
With a pistol in each hand he issued the
order, "Major, order your men to pick up
and carry in our wounded.   We ain't a

goin' to leave no good American doughboys out here in the forest to die." The Germans obeyed with alacrity, after which the major humanely inquired, "What about the German wounded?" The dead shot from the Tennessee mountains regarded this as a reflection upon his marksmanship, and promptly informed the German officer, "There hain't any." He knew he had not missed a shot. This was corroborated when the salvage corps and other details visited the grounds later that day.

For the first time in his life he was lost. He could not take his eyes off the prisoners in order to orient himself. He inquired, "Major, which way to the American lines?" The major, hoping to lead York into an ambush of machine gunners in the woods over on the left, pointed in that direction. The suspicious mountaineer, ever on the alert, exclaimed, "Ho, ho!" and immediately marched in the opposite direction.

After he had proceeded several hundred yards, he made the terrible discovery that he had not captured the German front line as he thought he had. The doughboys in going through the forest had actually penetrated through the front line and York had taken the second line, far behind. In order to get his prisoners out he had now to go through the front line, approaching it from the rear. He never even hesitated. He marched his column right at it. And when the machine gunners there reversed their weapons and began to fire, he pressed his pistol into the major's ribs and ordered, "Blow that thar whistle again, and blow it right smart." The major did so and the front line surrendered. One brave German refused to throw up his hands and continued to man his gun. York "teched him off" too. He collected about fifty more prisoners, added them to his column, and proceeded out across No Man's Land toward the American trenches. The intelligence officer, Joseph A. Woods, as stated in his affidavit, challenged him and counted the prisoners. He counted—one—two—three—four—ten—twenty—fifty—one hundred—and then, with a surprised look in his eyes, inquired, "Good Lord, have you captured the whole German army?"

The red-headed corporal grinned and replied, "I've got a tol'able few."

## Chapter XXIV

## "The Faith That Moveth Mountains"

CORPORAL YORK had to escort his prisoners ten miles behind the American lines to the French military police at Varennes. Chivalrously he allowed them, whenever it was possible, to take cover from their own artillery fire, which was concentrating on the roads behind the American lines. "Thar's been enough of you killed already," he told them.

He had been up all night, marching to the front lines; fighting and escorting prisoners all day; and it took him all the next night to rejoin his company, which in the meantime had cut the railroad and successfully taken all objectives.

He said nothing whatever about his heroic feat. When Captain Danforth asked him where he had been, he merely replied that he had been in a little fight. The captain reminded him that they had "all been in a little fight," and he could not understand why Corporal York had been away all the previous day. The red-headed mountaineer returned his captain's gaze and told him that he had some prisoners that he had to take back. The company commander rather warmly pointed out that he had issued strict instructions that prisoners were to be turned over to battalion headquarters and the doughboys were to return immediately to the front lines. He wanted to know why York had not obeyed this order.

"I done takened them to battalion headquarters and they told me they hadn't enough men available to take them over from me," was his quiet reply.

"You should have turned them over to brigade headquarters and then rejoined your command," admonished the captain.

"I done takened them to brigade headquarters and they ordered me back to divisional headquarters," answered the corporal.

The captain looked at him steadily for a moment. He knew York and knew him to be truthful. "In the name of God, how many prisoners did you have?"

When the big fellow answered, "One hundred and thirty-two," he gasped in amazement, "One hundred and thirty-two!"

Despite York's reticence in discussing the fight, it was too tremendous a feat of arms to keep hushed up. Some of the survivors passed the news along. Captain Danforth and Sergeant Parsons began to piece the story together. It spread like wildfire along the American front—a dough-boy, practically single-handed, had whipped a German machine-gun battalion.

York explained to the captain that he would like to have a couple of stretcher bearers to go back to the scene of the fight with him and search for any wounded who might be lying around in the brush. The request was granted immediately and the little detail combed the surrounding forest for hours. There were no wounded.

A few days later he was recommended for the Congressional Medal of Honor, promoted to sergeant and taken out of the front lines. Shortly afterwards the Armistice was signed.

After the Armistice, accompanied by staff officers and war correspondents, he returned to the battle field. The ground was carefully photographed and measured and his own affidavit and that of other eyewitnesses taken. The feat was so incredible that the officers could not believe it. They held investigation after investigation until every single doubt had been removed and every claim made on Sergeant York's behalf substantiated.

Colonel Richard Wetherill asked the mountaineer to march him out in exactly the same way he had marched out the German major and the prisoners. After York had done so, the colonel exclaimed, "It is not human for a man to do what you have done."

The war correspondents and officers pressed closer to hear his explanation. He was silent for a moment, and then quietly but firmly asserted that it was not human but Divine power that had directed and saved him that day. "I believed in God, and I done know He watched over me," he told them.

There was a brief pause. The colonel, with moist eyes and a catch in his voice, returned, "My boy, I think you are right."

His simple faith impressed even the most skeptical, and there was not a man present who did not acknowledge that perhaps after all the mountaineer knew what he was talking about.

Alvin York has never swerved in his belief that his God watched over him in the fight. He does not care to argue the point, nor does he insist that others share his belief. He won the fight. He came out of it unharmed. He is content to let it go at that.

A few days later a French motorcyclist driving him in a trailer to Army headquarters was burning up the road and doing nearly seventy miles an hour. The big fellow, after standing it as long as he could, made the driver stop, got out and commented, "You can expect too much of God." Humorous but sensible. He could not very well help himself in the awful fight with the machine guns and he called upon his God to protect him, but he could not see any sense in driving so fast over those rough French roads. His faith is simple, workable, and wholesome.

## CHAPTER XXV

## America's Tribute

YORK was awarded the Congressional Medal of Honor, the Croix de Guerre with palms, and over forty other high Allied decorations. General Pershing pronounced him "the outstanding civilian hero of the World War." The Allied commander in chief, Marshal Foch, eulogized him in these glowing words: "What you did was the greatest thing accomplished by any private soldier in all the armies of Europe."

Upon his return to New York City in May, 1919, he received the biggest reception ever given a home-coming American hero, with the single exception, of course, of the glorious Colonel Charles A. Lindbergh. The New Yorkers took one look at him and went wild with enthusiasm. His red hair, blue-gray eyes which looked straight into yours, picturesque dialect, and the lean, panther-like figure of the hunter and mountaineer appealed tremendously to their imagination.   The rumors of his deadly skill with the rifle, and most incredible of all, the fact that he had been three times a conscientious objector increased the interest.   Towering over everything else was the feat itself—he had whipped a German machine - gun battalion, killed twenty-eight Germans, captured thirty-five machine guns, and with the assistance of half a dozen doughboys brought in one hundred thirty-two prisoners.

The mountaineer who had lived in log cabins and caves on the mountain side, in small army huts and tents, in lousy dugouts and dirty trenches, was installed in a suite in one of the most luxurious hotels in the world.   Upon entering his bedroom, he saw twin beds for the first time in his life. He scratched his head, grinned, and commented, "They ain't a goin' to fool me nohow; I'm a goin' to sleep in both of 'em."

When he was offered twenty thousand dollars a week to appear in a revue with some seminude girls, he merely grinned and commented, "Wouldn't I look funny in tights, ho, ho!"

Altogether he was offered over a quarter of a million dollars to go on the stage, on the screen, and to sign advertisements. He positively refused to commercialize his fame, with the brief but pointed reply, "This here ole uniform of Uncle Sam's ain't for sale nohow." When they insisted, he told them to "keep their thirty pieces of silver."

He visited Washington, D. C., as a guest of the Secretary of War, and appeared in Congress, where both houses joined in giving him a tremendous ovation.

Upon his return to New York City he was invited on the floor of the Stock Exchange where the brokers temporarily postponed hostilities. He was given a great banquet at the Waldorf-Astoria with many of the most notable leaders in the nation present. They toasted and eulogized him for hours. Years later, commenting on this banquet, he said that they talked so much about him that he got tired inside of his head, and that he could hear "them thar hound dogs of mine a bayin' for me to come back."

He bore his honors with a becoming modesty and dignity, which quickly im-

16

pressed the people with the fact that he was not merely a war hero whose one claim to fame was that he was a dead shot, but that he was a truly great American imbued with a lofty patriotism and touched with the divine fire of genius.

He asked for nothing for himself. He refused all presents and rejected all offers of money. He positively would not sell out. He would, however, like a ride in the subway. How human and illuminating! The unsophisticated country boy wanted to see the wonder works of the big city. He wanted to ride underneath it.

A few days later he said good-by to the bright lights of Broadway and returned home to the little old log cabin in the Valley of the Three Forks of the Wolf and "them thar hound dogs of mine and the life where I belong."

There never was such a home-coming. The purest Anglo-Saxons in the world, speaking the language of Chaucer and Shakespeare—the men in jeans and overalls, "toting" muzzle-loaders, and the women in linsey dresses and split bonnets—turned out to welcome him.

When it was all over and the excitement had subsided a little, he put away his uniform, slipped into his overalls, took the old "rifle-gun" down from the wall, whistled to his "hound dogs" and went "a-huntin'— for Gracie. He done found her and he done married her."

He had traveled across the seas and been in many lands. He had met the beautiful women of the world. He could in all probability have had his choice of them, but he placed Gracie Williams above them all.

A few weeks later the Governor of Tennessee made him a colonel for life, and with his staff, in the presence of nearly five thousand people from all over America, married him on the mountain side, in the shadow of the log cabin that the Long Hunter had built over a century and a half ago, among the blue hills hallowed by the footsteps of David Crockett, Daniel Boone, big Sam Houston, and Old Hickory himself.

# Chapter XXVI

## Schools and Roads

THE little valley tucked away among the blue mountains looked very much the same. The mill dam sang as it used to sing before the war. The razorbacks grubbed for acorns as industriously and the bells around their necks jangled as tunefully as ever. The dogwood and the redbud blossomed on the hillside. The road to Pastor Pile's was just as rough as in 1917. Everything was very much as it had been then. Mother York looked scarcely a day older. The big red-headed brothers and sisters appeared about the same as usual. The World War had scarcely touched the little valley community.

Only Alvin had changed. It seemed like a dream. A year before he had been an unknown, illiterate mountaineer training as a private in the army. Now he was world-famous. From all over America came presents, offers of fortunes, wires and letters

(230)

Elementary Department of the York Agricultural School

of congratulation. The papers and magazines never tired of singing his praises. New decorations arrived in almost every mail.

The big fellow was puzzled. What was it all about? What was the meaning of it? Whither away? He knew that every war has to have its hero. He could not understand, though, why he happened to be the chosen one. He was not a regular army man nor even a volunteer. Most certainly he had not wanted to go. The authorities had drafted him against his will. Now, only a few months later, he was being unanimously chosen as the outstanding hero of the World War.

He slipped into his overalls, and with his muzzle-loader under his arm and his "hound dog" at his heels, tramped the mountains, away from everybody, where he could think things through. His faith inspired him to believe that there is a purpose in everything and that "mysterious are the ways of the Lord, His wonders to perform." He returned to the place on the mountain side where before going overseas he had prayed to God for guidance. Again he knelt and

held a lonely communion with his Maker,
who he sincerely believed had protected him
in the fiercest battles.  Simply and earnestly
he offered thanks.

Before the war he had never been out of
the mountains and had no idea of what the
outside world was like.  Now that he had
been in many parts of his own country and
had crossed the seas and visited other lands,
he seemed to see things differently.  Much
that he had witnessed did not appeal to
him.  Some few things made a lasting
impression.  For instance, he had never
realized what a terrible handicap in life it
is to be illiterate until he had mixed with
men and women who had what he called
"a heap o' larnin'."  He also compared, to
their disadvantage, the mountain trails and
creek beds in his country with the up-to-
date roads and highways he had seen in
his travels.

Here were two things which were good
and which would mean much to the mountain people—roads and schools.  He turned
them over in his mind.  He prayed often
and gradually began to understand.  The
mountaineers had remained behind the

times and without these wonderful things
far too long. The hour of the awakening
was at hand. Maybe he was meant to be
the leader. Maybe that is why his life had
been spared.

The county, the state, and the whole
nation were anxious to honor him in a
practical way. He wanted very little for
himself. He accepted with gratitude a
nice home and farm in the valley from the
Rotary Clubs. He refused everything else.

He traveled to Nashville and asked the
Commissioner of Highways to build a road
through the mountains. The request was
granted. Where there had been creek beds
and mountain trails, the York Highway was
constructed. That started things. The
counties on both sides contributed their
share and added many miles. Today you
can travel in comfort and safety along this
beautiful highway from Knoxville right
through the heart of the mountains to
Nashville.

Schools came next. The state voted fifty
thousand dollars and the county the same.
Loving friends and supporters throughout
America raised the amount to one hun-

dred fifteen thousand dollars.   With this money he built a high school on one side and a grade school on the other side of Jamestown, which is the county seat. They are modern schools with up-to-date equipment and the best teachers procurable. He secured some busses which travel fifteen miles up and down the highway and bring the children to school and take them back home again.   They are in the heart of the mountains, far from the nearest passenger railroad and forty miles from the nearest up-to-date schools.   They accommodate several hundred mountain boys and girls.

Plans are under way for "Moonlight Schools" for parents to attend on moonlight nights.   Later on there is to be an agricultural college.

Sergeant York's struggle to build these schools has been a harder fight than the one he fought in the Argonne.   The old order dies hard.   Ignorance gives ground slowly.   There has been trouble with the bankers and the lawyers and friction with local school boards.   It has been a hard, bitter fight.   But the man who never flinched before the German machine-gun battalion in the depths of the Argonne forest has never lost heart in his attempt to "bring a heap o' larnin' to the mountain boys and girls." The schools are functioning today. They are quasi-state institutions. The mountaineers are awakening. The big red-headed soldier from the Valley of the Three Forks of the Wolf is the recognized leader of the new movement.

Much remains to be done. There is still far too much illiteracy throughout the mountains. In his sparsely populated county alone there are over one thousand boys and girls between the ages of six and eighteen who cannot read and write. Schools must be provided for them, more schools, and more and more. Alvin York has dedicated his life to seeing that they are built.

## Chapter XXVII

# The Hero Who Made Good

IN the fall of 1929, over ten years after York's return to America, the War Department in Washington, D. C., staged a reproduction of his world-famous fight in the Argonne. The woods, trenches, and fox holes were reproduced. Regular Army men played the rôles of the German and American doughboys. Tens of thousands of patriotic Americans cheered as the soldier who played the part of Alvin York whipped and captured the German machine-gun battalion.

A few days later Alvin appeared in Congress and was given an ovation. This was one of the few times that the representatives of this country have twice acclaimed, on the floor of the House, an American hero. Coming eleven years after the feat which won him the Congressional Medal of Honor, it was a wonderful tribute to a hero who had made good. Alvin York has never commercialized his fame and has never done anything which has directly or indirectly brought anything but credit to his uniform. He has built schools and roads in the mountains and is gradually leading his people toward the life more abundant. Official Washington knew of this, and for the second time applauded him to the skies.

The hero's rôle is a difficult one. He is subjected at all times to the pitiless glare of publicity. His virtues and vices are at all times subject to distortion. He has only to make the slightest slip and his fame too often is gone forever.

The Lindberghs, the Byrds, and the Yorks have a tremendous load upon their shoulders. They bear the love and the trust of tens of millions of patriotic Americans. The younger generation especially watch their every movement. If ever they fall from grace, they will bring disappointment and disillusionment to millions of boys and girls throughout the nation. They never will, because they are of the real stuff of heroes.

Alvin Cullum York at the height of his fame was regarded as a sure-shooting mountaineer who had accomplished marvels with rifle and pistol. When he returned from France, he vanished quickly into the obscurity of the mountains. The public was prepared to remember him as a war hero—no more—no less.

As the years have rolled on and stories of his great achievements in the mountains have appeared in the press, the American public has begun to realize that here is one hero who is greater in peace than in war and who is today among the foremost living Americans. His modesty, his clean mode of living, his heroic work in building roads and schools, his spirituality and nobility of character, have slowly made their impression upon his fellow countrymen. He is better known today and more deeply loved than ever before. He is a legend while yet alive.

He is forty-three years of age and is much fleshier than he was when he went to war. The lean, lithe figure and the panther-like grace and swiftness of movement have gone. However, one has to talk with him for only a few moments to realize that the old fire is still there and burning more brightly than

High school built by Sergeant York in the mountains, forty miles from the nearest passenger railroad

ever before.  He lives on his farm in the valley with his beloved Gracie and his four boys: Alvin Jr., George Edward Buxton, Woodrow Wilson, and Andrew Jackson. Another little one, Sam Houston, passed away a few months ago.  "Gracie will never recover from it," he told me, with tears in his eyes.  He spends most of his time working on the farm, looking over his schools, and dreaming and planning others to be built in the future.  Occasionally he makes a trip North to tell the public of his plans.  He is just as unaffected and quiet today as he was before he went to war. The mountaineers hunt and shoot with him. They aways refer to him as "the Sergeant." He is still the greatest shot in the mountains.

The woman who answers the telephone in Jamestown, the county seat, is Mrs. Crockett, a descendant of the immortal Davy Crockett.  A few miles away across the mountains there is a tree marked:

|  | D. Boon |
|---|---|
| CillED | A. BAR |
| in | thE |
| yEAR | 1760 |

The spelling, punctuation, and arrangement are just as Boone placed them. Near by is the old house where Andrew Jackson used to stay on his way from Nashville to Washington. Abraham Lincoln was born less than two hundred miles away, over in Kentucky. This is the land of the pioneers of pioneers and of the Long Hunters. Alvin York is their lineal descendant. He is an eighteenth-century character living in the twentieth century, and has been fittingly referred to as "one of our contemporary ancestors." The mantle of Boone and Crockett, of Houston and "Old Hickory," has fallen on worthy shoulders in Alvin Cullum York, the Last of the Long Hunters.

# Give Attendance to Reading

"Paul has not lost his delight in books, even when he is near his death," said John Calvin. He alluded to Paul's counsel, "Give attendance to reading," written from his prison in Rome. Down to the moment that he prepared for death, Paul was still the book lover!

There is his touching message to Timothy as the aging apostle pleads, "The cloak that I left at Troaz with Carpus, when thou comest, bring with thee, and the books, but especially the parchments."

Paul leaves no doubt in any mind that Christian preachers and teachers ought to be readers.

Of course there is always the danger of reading too much and thinking too little. Too much reading, however, is not a fault that many American pastors have taken time to acquire.

A visiting English preacher observed: "In America every minister has a fine car and a television set. He seems always to be talking on the telephone or rushing somewhere. But your ministers do not have libraries. In England our clergy do not have fine cars and usually no telephone, but our ministers do have libraries."

"Sell your shirt and buy books," was a motto that helped make Scotland a land of great preachers.

But the truth is, many a minister simply cannot afford to buy the necessary books. Therefore, every church ought to put into its budget, each year, a substantial sum for the purchase of books for its pastor. If this is not made an item in the budget, as it ought to be, then his congregation ought to give the pastor money earmarked "for the purpose of books." Books will enrich his mind, illumine his soul, and enliven his preaching. "Much reading doth make a full man," said Bacon.

In this respect, Catholics are far more alert and logical than Protestants. A Catholic publishing house writes to every Catholic: "Dear Catholic Readers: Wish a merry Christmas the Catholic way. Give Catholic books to everyone. Catholic books are among the best books that offer something of your most precious possession — your faith."

Do not be surprised if your Catholic friends present you with a Catholic book. They are instructed to do so. Then why should not Protestants purchase and scatter books of the Gospel of redemption and of freedom among their friends, too.

The Communists make tremendous gains by promoting their books. It is time to scatter Christian books like the leaves of the autumn. When we buy a book on the Christian faith and give it to a non-believer, we are sending out a missionary. The Christian church must be a "propagandist society."

Lincoln is a classic example of what a few books can do to educate and inspire a humble personality into greatness. In youth Lincoln read the Bible through six times. It is difficult to imagine what the history of America might have been had not that blessed Book been available to the boy Lincoln.

What better counsel have we after nineteen hundred years than the dying Paul's admonition, "Give attendance to reading"?

Facts do not cease to exist because they are ignored.

Huxley

---

In my contact with people I find that, as a rule, it is only the little narrow people who live for themselves, who never read good books, who do not travel, who never open up their souls in a way to permit them to come into contact with other souls -with the great outside world.

Booker T. Washington
Tuskegee Institute

---

You can often learn a lot about a man's character by talking to his neighbors or to his business associates.

L.H.

---

Immortality

God may be a matter of indifference to the evolutionists, and a life beyond may have no charm for them, but the masses of mankind will continue to worship their Creator and continue to find comfort in the promise of their Savior that He has gone to prepare a place for them. Christ has made of death a narrow starlit ship between the companionship of yesterday and the reunion of tomorrow. Evolution strikes out the stars and deepens the gloom that enshrouds the tomb.

From Byran's Posthumous Speech

# SAVED THROUGH A TELEPHONE CONVERSATION

It really is great to know that when you die, you will go to Heaven. Before December 26, 1974, I didn't have the security of knowing this. I've always traveled a lot and at times I would think about what would happen to me if my car were to run off the road and crash and I were to die. I didn't want to think of death so I would start thinking about something else. On December 26, 1974 at 7:00 PM I accepted Jesus Christ as my personal Savior. I no longer fear death but instead I'm looking forward to spending eternity with Jesus in Heaven and also with my brother, who died on July 4, 1978, and my six-year old son, whom the Lord took in January, 1976.

I was reared on a small farm in central Mississippi and regularly attended the Baptist church a half mile away. I hardly ever missed a service, not because I enjoyed going, but because my mom and dad went and they made me go.

At the age of sixteen during a local revival and upon the insistence of my pastor and Mother, I joined the church and was baptized. Like so many people that are baptized today, I went down a dry sinner and came up a wet sinner because nobody had taken the Bible and showed me how I must repent of my sins and ask Jesus Christ to come into my heart and save me. After starting college, I rarely attended church, except when I went home and that was only to please my mother. After a year and a half of college, I entered military service and during basic training became a chapel guide in my squadron. I volunteered to do this because I felt I was religious enough and I also thought I might evade extra duty. While in Vietnam I went to church a few times, only because I felt I needed some religion to ease my conscience. About the only time I called on the Lord was when I was in trouble. Nobody had ever really witnessed to me about Heaven and Hell and although I had a small desire deep down inside to live a clean moral life, I was more interested in living a worldly life or as a beer advertiser calls it, "the good life."

After my discharge from the service, I reentered college. A year later my first marriage failed and I was free to join a fraternity and seek the pleasures of the social world. I had an apartment, sports car, friends, parties and all that goes with that life, including the emptiness. At this time my brother, Gary, was going to a Christian school in Indiana called Hyles-Anderson College. Every time he came home he would talk to me about being saved but I told him I was saved and that he should live his life and I would live mine. We were both home in Mississippi for the holidays in December, 1974 and I tried to avoid him because I knew what he was going to talk about. He finally persuaded me to listen to a tape by Evangelist J. Harold Smith called "God's Three Deadlines". I was getting convicted from listening to that tape and hoping something would happen to it and sure enough, it quit playing. "Well", I thought to myself, "that takes care of that . . ." But my brother didn't give up. He got on the phone and called a friend of his from Hammond, Indiana, who is now an evangelist and teacher named Johnny Pope. We talked for a few minutes and he asked me, "Larry, if you were to die this very minute do you know that you would go to Heaven?" I said "Well, I hope so but I really don't know for sure." He said that the Bible tells us that we can know for sure. He read me several verses from the book of Romans which made me realize that everyone is a sinner (Rom. 3:23), that the penalty for sin is death (Rom. 6:23), that Christ has already paid the penalty (Rom. 5:8), and that it is necessary to accept what Christ has done for us as one would accept a gift

(Rom. 10:13). He then said, "Larry, wouldn't you like to be saved tonight?" I thought about it for a few seconds and I knew I really hadn't been happy with my past life so I said okay. We bowed our heads and he prayed and I prayed and trusted Jesus Christ as my Savior. I didn't have an emotional experience and I really didn't feel any different but I knew I had made a commitment to the Lord, and the Bible says we are saved by grace, through faith in Christ, not by feelings. (Eph. 2:8,9).

Brother Pope told me to be sure to tell people that I got saved. Since mother had been crying and praying for me, I was glad to let her know that I had accepted the Lord, but she didn't think I meant it. I went back to where I was going to school, which was Southern Mississippi, and my roommate was swimming in the indoor pool. I went up to him and said, "Wes, guess what happened to me over the holidays! I got saved!" He replied, "That's great. I've been saved a long time myself." We had gone to parties and drank booze together and I certainly couldn't see Christ in his life. I decided that my life was going to be different because I was tired of straddling the fence as many so called Christians are doing. (II Cor. 5:17).

The following Sunday night I went to an independent Baptist church and Pastor C. R. Williams preached about the responsibility of Christians to lead others to Christ. I was assured in my heart and mind that I had been saved so, during the invitation, I walked the aisle and made a public profession of faith. I was baptized the next Sunday and started telling my friends I had been saved and began distributing gospel tracts. Everyone thought I had become a fanatic and they said that Harrison is just trying something new and that it wouldn't last. Well, Praise the Lord, it has been over four years now and Jesus becomes sweeter to me every day. Jesus Christ died on the cross and shed His precious blood so that we might have eternal life. I'm so thankful that the Lord allowed me to live twenty-seven years and that on that December night I dropped all pretense and opened my heart to Jesus Christ in simple faith.

*How about you?* On what do you base your hope of Heaven? A good life? Church membership? Perhaps you have been making the same mistake that I had made for so long. The Bible states, "Believe on the Lord Jesus Christ, and thou shalt be saved." (Acts 16:31). It is one thing to believe about a person but it is quite another thing to trust yourself to that person. I had always believed in Jesus Christ but I had never trusted him completely to take me to Heaven. There are many who believe the basic facts about the Lord Jesus Christ, (the Bible says the devils believe and tremble. [James 2:19],) but they have never committed themselves to Him. They believe He can save them but they do not let Him do it.

To believe in Christ is more than to believe historical facts about Him. It means you must turn your life over to Him and depend on Him entirely for your soul's salvation and for happiness in this life. It's a personal decision and only you can make it. Will you trust Him now and be saved for eternity? (John 5:24).

*LARRY HARRISON*

## MY DECISION

I have confessed my sins and to the best of my ability I have trusted Jesus Christ as my Lord and Savior for eternity.

# A GREAT HYMN STORY

Your pastor's favorite hymn has long been, "HOW FIRM A FOUNDATION" which we often sing.

There is evidence that it was written by Robert Keene, a song leader in a Baptist church in London.

It was the favorite hymn of Deborah Jackson, President Andrew Jackson's beloved wife, and on his death-bed the warrior and statesman called for it. It was the favorite of General Robert E. Lee, and was sung at his funeral.

"How firm a foundation, ye saints of the Lord,
    Is laid for your faith in His excellent Word!
What more can He say than to you He hath said,
    To you who for refuge to Jesus have fled?

"Fear not, I am with thee, O be not dismayed,
    For I am thy God, I will still give thee aid;
I'll strengthen thee, help thee, and cause thee to stand,
    Upheld by My gracious, omnipotent hand.

"When thro' the deep waters I call thee to go,
    The rivers of sorrow shall not overflow;
For I will be with thee thy trials to bless,
    And sanctify to thee thy deepest distress.

"When thro' fiery trials thy pathway shall lie,
    My grace, all-sufficient, shall be thy supply;
The flames shall not hurt thee, I only design
    Thy dross to consume, and thy gold to refine."

*(Three more great stanzas, too!)*